# THERE IS NO PRINCE

## And Other Truths
## Your Mother Never Told You

A Guide to Having the Relationship *You* Want

## What women who have taken the Workshop that inspired this book are saying ...

"After years of thinking I would just grow old and do good work, I took the workshop and now I've been in a relationship—a comfortable, wonderful, and very loving relationship—for four years. That just wouldn't have happened had it not been for the 'Having What You Want With a Man Workshop.'"

—Literary agent, age 58

"I've read all the other books and they're just so many words. This work actually gives women a vehicle, a technology, for turning their lives around. It not only makes sense, it works."—Corporate lawyer, age 42

"I realized that I don't have to live by someone else's expectations of what I should want in a man. I get to choose *for myself* based on what's authentic for me. I'm not in a new relationship yet, but I can already see how this work is affecting me in job situations with male bosses. When we drop our expectations that men will behave like women, all our relationships are *a lot easier.*"

—Office manager, age 26

"I always thought I'd have to settle and have things that I didn't want [in a man and in a relationship]. But I didn't want to settle, so for years I just haven't been in a relationship. The workshop gave me a whole new perspective on who I am and what I desire *and* who men are. I feel so much more empowered now to have my own feelings, judgments, and intuitions. Now I can actually dare to dream of what I want." —Television producer, age 47

"It was so reassuring looking around and seeing all these attractive, successful women who were having the same issues with men. Just knowing that there's something systemic to it and that we weren't given the right information about men has been helpful. I also realized how much *I* had to do with not having a man in my life. I had a lot to clear away. Before the workshop I would have never seen my husband—*would have never even seen him*—sitting right there next to me."—Ad executive, age 41

"In the workshop we talked about lists—having lists of what's good for us and what we *must have* in a man and in a relationship. These lists have really helped me attract the kind of men who would be good for me and they have also saved me from being with men who weren't good for me. This surely has saved me great heartache."—Financial analyst, age 35

"The workshop allowed me to see what I put in my own way—and how I was carrying certain unconscious thoughts that were causing me to react in ways that didn't work. Whether with a man or in any kind of relationship, this has helped me to think differently and get out of my own way."

—**Retail manager, age 32**

"One of the greatest things I learned in the workshop was that there simply doesn't have to be a battle of the sexes. I learned to own my power, to use my female power and not feel manipulated. I don't feel like a victim anymore. Realizing that men are not the enemy makes for peace, and peace makes for happiness. This has helped me tremendously."—**Graphic artist, age 29**

"The workshop really helped me expand my relationship with my *self*. From a place of self-love I can have what I want in all my relationships—with a man or in a work environment or with friends."—**Executive assistant, age 39**

"It's nice to know that men and women are *supposed* to be different!"

—**Artist, age 23**

"Before I did the workshop, I always blamed men for going away. Now I get it that I have something to do with it. I realize that although I've always said I *have*, I really *haven't* wanted to be in relationship."—**Photographer, age 64**

"The workshop actually healed my relationships with women. It made me appreciate women like I never did before. I also started noticing men, men, and more men. I realized that when I'm not looking for a prince, all these men just appear! Pretty amazing."—**Club manager, age 32**

"I never saw men as human beings. Now I can. I feel so much more compassion for men, even though they're so different from women. At Life Works I learned to have compassion and an open heart toward men."

—**Freelance designer, age 55**

"I felt a softening toward myself and other people, especially men. I realized how much I stand in my own way and learned not to judge myself for it."

—**Retired teacher, age 68**

"This work has truly transformed me, which in turn has changed the types of men I attract. I'm just much more able to have come my way the kind of man I really want."

—**Office manager, age 46**

"I see a river of hope that I've never seen before. There seems to be light there."

—**Divorced mother and government worker, age 53**

**Also by the authors**

The Female Power Within

A Guide to Living a Gentler, More Meaningful Life

# THERE IS NO PRINCE

## And Other Truths
## Your Mother Never Told You

A Guide to Having the Relationship *You* Want

Marilyn Graman and Maureen Walsh
*with Hillary Welles*

L·I·F·E
WORKS
BOOKS

New York

Life Works Books
55 Fifth Avenue – Penthouse
New York, NY 10003, U.S.A.
212-741-8787  fax 212-741-9242
www.lifeworksbooks.com

This publication is designed to provide accurate and authoritative information in regard to the subject matter covered. It is sold with the understanding that the publisher is not engaged in rendering legal, accounting, or other professional service. If legal advice or other expert assistance is required, the services of a competent professional should be sought.—*From a Declaration of Principles Jointly Adopted by a Committee of the American Bar Association and a Committee of Publishers and Associations*

Names of persons used in stories and examples have been changed to protect the person's privacy. Any similarity to any known persons living or dead is purely coincidental.

Cataloging in Publication by Santa Fe Public Library. Library of Congress CIP pending.

Graman, Marilyn.
      There is no prince and other truths your mother never told you :
      a guide to having the relationship you want / Marilyn Graman and
      Maureen Walsh, with Hillary Welles
      1st ed.
      New York : Life Works Books
      p. cm.
      ISBN 0-9718548-7-4

      1.Man-woman relationships. 2.Intimacy (Psychology). 3.Mate selection.
      I. Walsh, Maureen. II. Welles, Hillary. III. Title: No prince.
      306.7—dc21

LCCN 2002096259

Cover design by John Buse

Page design by Jason Gray

Illustration by Paul Manchester

Printed on acid-free paper in the United States of America.

2 3 4 5 6 7 8 9 10     First Edition 2003

For all the women known and yet to come
   who by their use of the information contained here
   have more love in their lives

# CONTENTS

# PREFACE

I was standing on the corner of Fifth Avenue and Eighth Street in the Village on a beautiful April morning when a car honked at me and the person in the passenger seat waved. Though I wasn't sure who it was, I waved back. Partway down the block the car backed up and stopped in a bus zone. Out of the car popped a familiar-looking woman. She opened the door behind her, taking a baby out of a car seat while the driver came around to join her. The woman strode toward me with a little girl on her hip, followed by the driver who was clearly the toddler's father. Although I couldn't recall the woman's name, I suddenly recognized her as having sat on the left side of the room in our "Having What You Want With a Man" Workshop a couple of years before.

"Marilyn, please forgive me. I'm such a terrible letter writer, so when I saw you I had to stop and thank you. I sent you a wedding invitation and a picture after I got married. My friend Sophia who did the Workshop later told me she saw it on the office bulletin board at Life Works. But then after Steffie was born eleven months later, I always meant to write you a note to tell you how much that weekend changed my life."

"I'm so glad for you. It makes my day when I hear that women are using what they learned in the workshop," I said. My heart swelled with gratitude for all the women who had put themselves in my hands at my workshops.

Her husband thrust his hand forward to shake mine. "You changed my life too, Marilyn. I want to thank you for the work you did with Marion. I met her two months after she did your course. She quotes you often, as if you're a family member. I feel like I know you and you're a fairy godmother in our lives." He hugged her close to him. "You know, I'd been looking for Marion for a long time." Our eyes misted over with the deep feeling he had just touched in us all—there at the corner of Fifth Avenue and Eighth Street.

A rose is itself
and the bee comes.

# INTRODUCTION

Every woman deserves a man who can stand behind her and applaud as she blossoms. She deserves a man who can be a best friend, consort, cheerleader, listener, cuddler, financial partner, father to her children, companion, and fellow traveler—a man who is an asset to her life. Every woman deserves to have a man who supports her and cherishes her. She deserves her own life, one she shares with a man she loves. She deserves to create the balance that works for her—and to choose the man and the relationship she desires. In short, every woman deserves to have the relationship she wants.

If you're wondering why you don't already have what you want, you are in good company. Millions of intelligent, successful women like you have been asking themselves the same question. So many of us have been putting our energy into making new choices and finding what's authentic for us. We've been building careers and perhaps putting off marriage and family for later —until one morning we wake up to find that "later" has arrived. Or we've had our hearts broken so many times it just seems hopeless or too much trouble to even put ourselves out there anymore.

Too many women think there's something wrong with them because they don't have the relationship they've always dreamed of. Listen. *There's nothing wrong with you!* You've just been given wrong information. It's as if you've lost your keys to having a good relationship in the grass but were told to look for them on the sidewalk because that's where the streetlight is shining. No amount of looking on that sidewalk is going to help you find your keys. No. You have to learn to look somewhere else. Look where no one told you to look before.

The focus of this book is to help you figure out how to see into that new place, to find what is uniquely true for you, and how to have the relationship *you* want. We want to cheer you on as your perceptions shift and you awaken to notice all the available *and* desirable men, sometimes right under your nose, who want to love and cherish and support you, who share your deepest values and beliefs, who can be your hero, your best friend, your fabulous lover *and* give you all the space you need to maintain the balance in your life that works best for you. There may not be any princes, but there are plenty of wonderful men out there just waiting for a woman like you.

Over the past few decades, women have made incredible breakthroughs in the areas of career, politics, and just generally choosing what their lives will look like. We have come a long way toward having what we want in so many new areas of our lives. Yet we are still trying to figure out who we are supposed to be in a relationship. Can we have a successful career *and* a successful relationship? Do we have to give up our careers to have a man? Is it okay to want to stay home and have children? Is it possible to be independent and also have a man in our lives? These are the relevant questions women everywhere are asking today *and* the reason so many of us don't have what we want with a man.

We have options our mothers and grandmothers never dreamed of. But nobody taught us how to be choice-makers. We don't have a blueprint for how to be in a relationship, how to heal decades of heartbreak, when to have a family, and how to balance home and career. Nobody taught us how to be independent *and* have a loving, supportive relationship. We were trained to surrender into a relationship and make a man the center of our lives. Then the women's movement showed up, and although we now have some other ways to live, that early training is still with us.

No matter what your mother told you, the truth is that there is no right way to have a relationship. You get to decide what you want—and yes, you *can* have it. You *can* have a great marriage—with or without kids. You can pool your money or keep it separate from his. You can choose to spend a few nights a week taking classes or going out with friends, or you can spend all your free time with your man. You can live in community with other families. You can let go of your career to tend the home fires or make more money than your husband or share a home-based business with him. And you can choose a man who really wants to be with a woman just like you. But in order to *have* what you want with a man you have to *know* what you want, and that starts with having a loving relationship with yourself.

Women have been conditioned to love others, but we're not always as good at loving ourselves, and not always aware of the ways we keep ourselves from having the things we say we want.

When we're self-loving, we let things take the time they need to instead of rushing into relationships to avoid being lonely. We have compassion for ourselves. We know how much space we need and how much closeness. We know what is acceptable *to us* and where to set limits. We know how much time we want to spend on our careers and how much with the man in our lives. And, perhaps most importantly, we realize that we can create full, rich lives—with or without a relationship.

Learning how to become so self-loving and so awake that the man who can love you best just walks into your life—that's what this book is all about. Wherever you are along the relationship continuum, this book is for you. It's for you if you are single—whether you are not currently dating, haven't dated for a long time, or are thinking about dating. It's for you if you are reading the personals or surfing the Internet, if you're actively meeting men, or if you're tired of dating. It's for you if you're seeing many men or if you're exclusive with one. This book is for you if you're having a relationship—whether it's one that is not committed or one that is. It's for you if you're married or living with a man or if your relationship needs help or is in trouble. It's for you if you're divorced or widowed. The truth is, you can have the relationship you want from wherever you are—whether that means getting off the couch and meeting a man, giving up a man who's not good for you, sampling a lot of men to know who's out there, deciding whether you want to commit to the man you're with, or making a shift within yourself so your marriage can be better.

## Who We Are

We have been helping women have what they want with men for over fifteen years. At our Life Works office in New York, our bulletin board is covered with photographs and letters from women who have taken our weekend-long "Having What You Want With a Man" Workshop and then found husbands or partners. Their letters and photographs express how much their hearts and lives have opened through what they learned. We wrote this book so that women everywhere would have the opportunity to experience heart-opening shifts like theirs.

After women complete the weekend course, many join a Relationship Support Group which is our weekly session to help them continue to explore and practice what they learned and uncovered in the Workshop. Additionally, they are offered the opportunity to work with a woman who has been trained in the Life Works points of view and information for at least three rigorous years. These sessions are a combination of listening, clearing, guiding, and sometimes coaching and cheerleading. Because of the delicate and intense nature of their work, we created a new title for this process. The work they do is called Guiding and the practitioners are called Guidesses.

Women who have participated in our workshops contributed all the stories in this book. Their names and identifying details have been changed to protect their privacy. "We" refers to Marilyn Graman, a psychotherapist who designs and delivers most of our courses, and Maureen Walsh, a producer at heart, who guides the development of new projects, creates and delivers specialized courses, and is the business side of Life Works. As in our last book, *The Female Power Within*, writer Hillary Welles brings the perspective of a younger generation.

## How to Use This Book

There is no formula or prescription in this book. All that is required is a willingness to become more aware—to use our information and make it your own.

This book will help you understand *why you have what you have* and *what you want and how to have it*. It will also give you a new appreciation of men. As you read, your perception of men and relationships will shift. You will no longer blame yourself or the men in your life for what's happened in the past, and you will be more optimistic that your future can be different from your past.

The next 13 chapters take you through the process we teach at our "Having What You Want With a Man" weekends. As you read, images and memories will come to you. Your mind will make interesting connections you may not have noticed before. Imagine that you have a room in your mind full of file cabinets. They contain all the experiences you've had in your life, what you decided because of them, and what you felt about yourself each time. Many of these files have been in deep storage, and you might not even be aware they exist. Yet, as you think about how you came to be who you are now, you can trust that the right file drawer will slide open and the right file will appear.

When a file opens it is often in the form of random thoughts. It is important to pay attention to your files because they offer important clues about why your life is the way it is. We suggest that you get a notebook and carry it with you so you can record the thoughts as they come up.

Everything you need to know is included in these chapters. If you want to go deeper, you can also do the exercises at the back of the book, which are organized to correspond to the chapters. The exercises help you discover how this work applies to *your* life. There are a few things to remember as you begin:

1. *Don't make changes right away.* This work will touch you at a deep level and some of it will happen unconsciously even after you've

finished the book. Putting off major changes is wise because it gives you time to integrate your new knowledge. We usually suggest that women wait three weeks after taking our workshop or reading this book before making any major changes in their lives.

2. *Try it on.* Sometimes the information you read may have you feeling stimulated, challenged, or sleepy. When this happens, it's a good idea to let yourself pause and ponder how the information is affecting you. You might automatically agree with some of the information and other points may pose a difficulty for you. If you don't agree with something, try it on for a while. You may discover that it has some wisdom for you. The information in this book is based on years of experience with thousands of women. If it is true for them, there is a good chance it might be true for you.

3. *Try to stop looking for the exceptions.* The things we tell you are true—except for sometimes. There are always exceptions, yet focusing on the exceptions is counterproductive. If we say, "Men want to make us happy," for example, we know it is not true for every situation or every man. Know that we are speaking in generalities and keep that in mind without dwelling on the exceptions.

4. *Be kind to yourself.* You are human and being human means you don't always get it right the first time. It's a trial-and-error universe and you are doing the best you can. Let yourself feel compassion for your struggle, and don't hold it against yourself that you don't have it all figured out yet.

5. *Be willing to be wrong.* We all hate being wrong. Yet if you'd been right about everything until now, you would already have what you want with a man. If you find yourself arguing with what you're reading, remind yourself that being wrong is good news because it means things don't have to be the way they've been. Making us right means you can have something different than what you've always had.

6. *Lean back and smile.* When you lean back, your view is broader and you can open your arms to let in new information. Sit somewhere comfortable and allow yourself to relax as you read. A little humor can go a long way, too.

7. *Expect regret.* As you explore your past, you may experience regret. It's natural to feel sad about things you wish you'd done and didn't do, or about things you wish you hadn't done but did. It's healthy to let yourself feel the sadness. Suppressing it will only hold you back from healing. Allow yourself to breathe into the feeling, welcoming it as a necessary step toward having what you want.

8. *Allow things to take the time they take.* Your mind can conceive of change in an instant but it takes time for change to happen in real life. Having what you want with a man may not happen overnight, and cultivating patience will help you to be aware of each step in the process.

9. *Look for what's working.* It's easy to notice big changes, yet our work is often subtle. It's the accumulation of small changes that allows your life to be different. Be open to noticing how you're doing things differently, or how men may be treating you differently. Give yourself lots of praise for the work you're doing.

10. *Make the information your own.* This is not a book of rules. We are making suggestions based on our experience. We know what generally works. The information is here to help you in whatever way you choose to use it. Every woman uses her new understanding in her own way.

11. *Expect to feel good about yourself—to feel relieved, refreshed, and have your life look different to you.* As you read this book you will be able to relax into your life knowing that what you want is coming to you. It *will* happen—it's just a matter of time. You can have what you want—once you are clear about what that is. You can create a relationship that is good *to* you and good *for* you. You can choose what you want based on the wisdom you've gained.

By the time you finish reading this book, your world will have changed. You will think differently, feel differently, approach things differently, and see yourself and men differently. You'll still recognize yourself in the mirror, but you might have a new glow because your new relationship to yourself is opening you up to having all kinds of wonderful new things happen in your life. Your load will have lightened. You will have answers to questions that have plagued women since we were cave dwellers. You will see that it is up to you to love yourself and choose men who are right for you. And you will have the very tools you need to have what you want with a man, starting today.

## *T*hink about...

 **What do you want a man for?**

*The exercises for the Introduction can be found on page 260.*

# CHAPTER ONE

## *There Is No Prince*

"*I've been single long enough,*" Jillian wrote on the first page of her new spiral-bound notebook. "*I am ready to find out how to have a great relationship with a man.*" Suddenly she felt the same kind of giddy anticipation she'd felt in college when she sat in a classroom at the beginning of the semester. She leaned back expectantly. Marilyn Graman entered the room and stood in front of the group of women. Smiling, she looked around and said, "Welcome to 'Having What You Want With a Man.' Congratulations for getting yourself here. Sometimes that's the hardest part."

"*Hard to get myself here?*" wrote Jillian. "*It took me years—and I still almost didn't come today! All I've had is lousy relationships—with me going back and forth between wanting to be married and promising to stay single forever.*"

Jillian could be any of the thousands of women who have come to our weekend-long relationship workshop. We call our course "Having What You Want With a Man."

Notice that we call it, '*having* what you want *with* a man.' Lots of women come to our workshop thinking that it is all about *getting* what they want *from* a man, but we're not about teaching any new tricks. When you take our course, you begin to think differently, feel differently, and approach things differently—about yourself, about men, and about relationships. Our book is designed to bring you the same results. As you read, you will discover that there are as many ways to be in relationships as there are women, and that you get to choose the kind of man and relationship you want. It's a relief to find that out, isn't it?

This book is designed to help you understand yourself better and understand men better. It will give you a new bridge between your past and the future you want. We all need that bridge, because somehow the future always does end up looking like the past. This book can help you make the changes you need to have something different in your life.

Congratulations on picking up this book. You have just begun your journey to the future—and the relationship—you want.

As Marilyn continued to speak, Jillian began to feel more relaxed.

"Why do you keep doing what you've always done? Because your images of how life can be are based on the past. Really making changes means going into the unknown—creating new pictures based on what you really want. And to do that you will want to clear away old ideas and patterns that don't help you. You'll need to separate yourself from your history and do something different from what you've always done."

> You learned *everything* you know about men and relationships when you were very young —and those first experiences are still running your life right now.

"*Clear away past junk,*" Jillian wrote in her notebook. "*Sounds good!*"

"The first thing you need to know if you want things to be different is this: *We all repeat our history over and over.* You learned *everything* you know about men and relationships when you were very young—and those first experiences are still running your life right now."

Marilyn paused as a ripple ran through the room. "Now I know you've learned a lot since your childhood, but listen to me. *Your early experiences are still running your life.* Just try out the idea for a while. I promise you that if you "make me right," that is, if you try on my point of view, and if you are willing to release the threads that are binding you to the past, you will have the opportunity to have what you want with a man."

"*Make Marilyn right*," Jillian jotted down, though with some hesitation. "*Okay, will try. ??? Done lots of work and just don't see how childhood still matters. Will keep open mind, keep listening.*"

"You were influenced about relationship in two ways when you were a child," Marilyn continued. "Number one was by the culture and the time period you grew up in. The norms, stereotypes, and expectations of our society taught you what your relationship should look like. You got those messages mainly from movies, television, magazines, books, and songs. They gave you an idealized version of relationships that no one could live up to—think Grace Kelly or Lady Diana and their "fairy-tale" marriages to Princes.

"Number two was by your family. While the culture was giving you messages about the ideal relationship you *should* have, your parents or the adults who raised you were modeling what a *real* relationship was like. And that was probably really different from the Hollywood or romance novel version of relationship, right?"

Murmurs of assent swept through the room.

"So the models for relationship you were given as a child were unrealistic, fairy-tale Hollywood relationships—and your parents' relationship, which had its own problems."

Jillian wrote, "*Hollywood=unrealistic, parents=too depressing.*"

"Now you've probably been wondering why on earth an attractive, intelligent woman like you doesn't have the terrific relationship she wants," said Marilyn. "And I'll bet you've come up with one of two answers—'There's something wrong with me,' or 'There are no good men out there.' Or both. Those are the answers women tend to end up with after years of disappointment in relationships. But I am here to tell you the good news.

"The good news is that there is nothing wrong with you, and there are plenty of good men out there. The reason you aren't in a great relationship, or the one you've always wanted, is not that you've got some kind of fatal flaw or that all the good men are taken. It's simply that *you were never taught how to have what you want with a man.*

"As a child you got handed a lot of wrong, unhelpful, and conflicting information from the media *and* from your parents—and then you were told to go out and find happiness with a man. It's as if you were shoved out of an airplane by a skydiving instructor, but instead of a parachute, she shoved you out with a pack full of dirty laundry. You couldn't possibly have a successful experience—yet you think there's something wrong with you because you're not floating happily through the air."

*"There is nothing wrong with me, and there are plenty of good men out there. Have been given wrong information,"* Jillian wrote, underlining it in red ink. *"Maybe this means it's not my fault I've never had the relationship I wanted???"*

"We were taught what our relationships *ought* to be like from movies, television, books, songs, and magazines— and we learned what our relationships *would* be like from our parents. And much of what we learned has been unhelpful. Not only does it provide us with unhealthy or unrealistic role models, but the messages are outdated. The culture has shifted greatly in the past forty years, and what we learned as children no longer matches up to the reality of everyday life. Women's roles have changed, and what women want and need in a relationship has also changed.

"It's really unfortunate and unfair that you were handed all this wrong information," Marilyn went on. "When you can ex-

> You were never taught how to have what you want with a man.

> We were taught what our relationships *ought* to be like from movies, television, books, songs, and magazines—and we learned what our relationships *would* be like from our parents.

plore your past and find out what you learned back then, it will help you see why you have the relationship you have today. If you're single, understanding what you learned in your past will help explain why. And when you understand *why* you have what you have today, you will have the power to change it.

"Before you can change what you have, though, it is absolutely crucial to understand how powerfully you have been repeating your history. You are living with certain expectations about relationship based on what you learned as a child. You anticipate that a man or a relationship will be a certain way, and your assumptions keep you from seeing what is really there. It's like your history provided you with glasses that only let you see certain kinds of people or situations. What you expect is what you get—it's practically a law of nature. If you expect men to be distant, for instance, you may attract men who are very busy with work or who live out of town. And the woman sitting next to you expects something else based on what *she* was taught. It's amazing how much what we expect comes into our lives. So I am saying to you that it is almost impossible to overestimate the influence your history has on what you have in your life right now."

*"What you expect is what you get,"* Jillian scrawled, underlining in red. *"Oh no!"*

"We will talk about your family history in a little while," said Marilyn. "Right now I want to focus on our shared cultural history—what we were taught about relationships by movies, television, magazines, books, and songs. I'm going to start out with a modern fairy tale that will illustrate what I'm talking about.

*✍♥*

**What you expect is what you get.**

*✍♥*

"Once upon a time there was a Martian named Oona who decided she wanted to travel to Earth and discover what it was like to be human. She went to the Elders of Mars to ask if she could travel to Earth for a while, and after much debate they decided to let her go.

"Before she left, the Elders spent a lot of time telling Oona how to survive as a human. They taught her that humans need certain fuels to keep them alive. One is called *food*. The other, they explained, is a green fluid called *water*. Whenever she felt an empty sensation in her middle, which humans called *hunger*, she would need to ingest some food. The Elders explained to Oona that there was a great variety of food, and told her where to get it and how it would look and smell. Whenever she felt a dry sensation in her throat, which the humans called *thirst*, she would need to drink the green fluid called *water*. So Oona went off, confident that she would survive with the good instructions her Elders had given her.

"Oona landed safely on Earth and spent the first few hours wandering around in a daze. After a while she started to feel tired and her middle ached. 'What is wrong with me?' she wondered. Then she remembered that this was her signal to find food. She found a place called a *supermarket* and paid for something called *bread*, and once she had chewed it and swallowed enough times the empty feeling in her middle went away and she felt energized.

"By the end of the afternoon Oona felt a strange sensation in her throat and her head started to ache. 'Oh,' she thought to herself, 'I must be experiencing what is known as thirst. It is just as the Elders said—first I was hungry and I ate food and I felt better, and now I am thirsty and I must find some of that green liquid called water to cure this dryness and this headache.' She went back to the supermarket and asked a man in a red apron where to find the water. He led her to an aisle filled with bottles of clear liquid.

"'No, I need the green water,' Oona explained to the man.

"'Lady, I don't know what you're talking about. Water isn't green, it's clear,' said the man and walked away.

"Oona left the supermarket feeling weak," continued Marilyn. "She walked all day and all night, and all the next day and the next night, but she couldn't find green water anywhere. Everywhere she asked for water they showed her the clear stuff, and yet she knew she could only drink green water because the Elders had told her so."

Marilyn paused and took a sip from her own glass of water. "Clear," she commented with a wry smile, prompting titters around the room.

*"Note to self: Water is clear and not green,"* Jillian wrote with her green pen. *"But what does this have to do with anything?"*

"After three days of searching, Oona couldn't walk anymore. She lay down on a bench, feeling so weak she didn't even care if she could find the green water. She fell asleep, and in her dream a beautiful woman in a flowing gown waved a sparkling wand and spoke to her in a silvery voice.

"'Oona, the Elders were wrong,' whispered the mysterious woman. 'I know that is hard for you to believe because they are supposed to know everything, but if you want to survive you have to believe me. Water is not green, it's clear. And if you drink some soon your human body will live. If you hold out for the green water, you will die.'

"Oona tossed and turned in a fitful sleep. 'I don't believe you,' she said. 'How could water be clear when the Elders told me it would be green? They've always been right before.'

"'Trust me,' said the shimmery woman. 'Be willing to be mistaken about this one thing you learned from the elders, and you will survive.' She waved her wand and disappeared.

"When Oona awoke she felt so awful that she could barely sit up. She decided that she had to believe the woman in her dream even though it meant going against everything she'd learned. She went to the supermarket and gave the man in the red apron some paper bills for a large bottle of the clear liquid he claimed was water, and though she was afraid she unscrewed the cap and took a long drink. Miraculously, she began to feel better. She took another drink, and felt instantly stronger.

"After drinking the entire bottle Oona felt ready for anything, and yet she was disturbed. The Elders *had* given her the wrong information. She decided to be more careful from then on and discover for herself what it really meant to be a human. And she lived happily ever after ... realizing that what she was taught was not necessarily the truth, making many mistakes, and learning all the time."

Jillian was scribbling as fast as she could. *"Aha! Green water is the wrong information—elders were wrong!"*

"So," Marilyn clasped her hands and held them to her heart, "like Oona, we have all been given a lot of wrong information that has caused us pain. It's hard to believe it is wrong because it's so ingrained in us and was given to us by supposed authorities. Once we can see that the truth is different from what we were told, though, we can start to see why we haven't had what we wanted.

"When you were a child you were trying to make sense of life all the time. You didn't have a fairy godmother who whispered explanations into your ear like Oona did. You had to figure it out by yourself, and you got your information from the culture and the family that raised you. So now I am going to play the part of your fairy godmother. I am going to help you by telling you the truth."

Marilyn glanced at her watch. "Why don't we take a two-minute stretch break?" she suggested.

Jillian stood and stretched her hands above her head. She felt curiously light and floaty, as if her sense of reality were shifting somehow. She sat down again and put her notebook in her lap. Her pen was poised, but she wasn't sure what to write yet.

*Your mother never told you...*
*that you were given the wrong information*
*about men and relationships.*

### Reality check

A hush fell over the assembled women as Marilyn took her seat again.

"Like Oona, you have been misled," Marilyn began. "You were told water is green and you have been diligently searching for green water, not realizing that you're looking for the wrong thing. In case you hadn't guessed, the green water represents the perfect man you were promised—the man who would provide everything you want exactly when you want it. The man who would be unfailingly romantic and attentive, and who would know what would make you happy without having to be told. The man who would be kind, nurturing, sweet, masculine, strong, handsome, considerate, gallant, and gentlemanly. In short—you have been promised a Prince.

"*Snow White, Cinderella,* and *Sleeping Beauty* taught you that you ought to wait for a Prince to make your life complete. Yet the Prince is a fabrication based on the ideals of chivalry, gentlemanly conduct, and fairy-tale endings. You didn't know this when you were a child trying to make sense of life. The Prince was presented to you as real and you trustingly followed what you were told. Like Oona waiting for the green water even though lots of clear water was available, you have been passing over a lot of fine, decent, caring human males because you are waiting for the perfect man, the ideal man, the knight in shining armor … Prince Charming. And you have been suffering, haven't you? You've been thinking that there is something wrong with you because you haven't found the Prince yet—and you might feel like you are dying of thirst."

*ℒ♥*

> You have been passing over a lot of fine, decent, caring human males because you are waiting for the perfect man, the ideal man, the knight in shining armor …Prince Charming.

*ℒ♥*

"*Waiting for a Prince,*" Jillian wrote with a purple pen. "*I thought Ernie was one until he forgot my birthday and left empty soda cans all over my apartment…*"

"The reality is that there are plenty of decent, kind, caring men who want relationships with women just like you—and you, and you," continued Marilyn, making eye contact with each woman in turn. "And once you can look at what's happening in your life in the light of what you learned as a child, you begin to create an opening for a man to come into your life. When you stop waiting for the Prince to come and whisk you off on his white steed, you can start seeing all the interesting, *interested* men who are all around you. But first you have to accept the fact that

## There is NO PRINCE."

Marilyn paused and repeated, "There is NO PRINCE."

Jillian scrawled, *"No Prince!!! Ack—is that true? What about my friend Carol's husband? He's so good-looking and even watches the kids sometimes. What about that guy I met at Caroline's? Wait . . . I want one! Not sure I want a real live man who can't save me with a kiss! Couldn't there be just one Prince? What about Jackson, the guy I met at the mayor's ball. He's so tall, dark, handsome, charming . . . Maybe he's the only Prince—and I found him—"*

## "There is NO PRINCE."

Marilyn reiterated as if in answer to Jillian's question. "As long as you are waiting for a Prince you are bound to be disappointed over and over again. A man can *look* like the Prince at first. You see him across a crowded room and he's handsome, witty, and charming. Yet once you get into a relationship with him you always find out that he is a human male with his own problems, idiosyncrasies, insecurities, and fears...and you feel cheated.

"Then you start thinking maybe there is something wrong with you because it looks like other women have found their Prince, and you don't have one of your own. You may not realize that your friends haven't found Princes either. They've found human males and simply accepted that they're not Princes after all. They *know* they haven't found a Prince because they are dealing with their men's human foibles, habits, and moods all the time. These men may act princely sometimes when the women in their lives are open to receiving what they have to offer, but there is NO PRINCE. If you see a man who looks like a Prince, talk to his ex-wife—she'll let you know exactly how he's not the Prince. Even Princess Diana didn't consider Charles a Prince.

**We just got the wrong information, that's all.**

"It's tragic when we start thinking there is something wrong with us because we don't have a Prince. We just got the wrong information, that's all. I hope

it is huge relief to know that it's not your fault. You were brought up believing in something that isn't real. You didn't have a fairy godmother to take you aside at the age of five and explain that everything you were watching, listening to, and reading was based on wishful thinking and that your idea of romance was based on an ideal that simply doesn't exist. So *I'm* being your fairy godmother now and telling you…

"There is NO PRINCE.

"Not anywhere.

"No man—not one."

*Your mother never told you…*
*that there is NO PRINCE.*

## *Think about…*

**How knowing that there is NO PRINCE opens you to seeing men differently.**

*The exercises for Chapter One can be found on page 261.*

# CHAPTER
## TWO

# *What You Were Taught About Men*

*"I can't believe I've been waiting for a nonexistent Prince,"* Jillian wrote in black ink after absorbing Marilyn's words. *"After all, I'm an enlightened twenty-first century woman!"*

Jillian isn't the only one who was waiting for a Prince. On some level, we are *all* waiting for a fairy-tale ending. If you were like most little girls, some of the first movies you saw were Disney's version of fairy tales. These movies caused a lot of mischief for little girls the world over as we absorbed the messages of the movies into our hearts. Cinderella was impossibly good, but that wasn't enough to save her from a life of drudgery. Sleeping Beauty was beautiful and sweet, but that wasn't enough to save her from the evil Maleficent's curse. Prince Charming, of course, was the one to save the day and the girl. Today, because of the awareness raised by the women's movement, it is easy to see the unhealthy pattern being set up—but as a four, six, or eight-year-old, you learned it well. And if you think about it, you'll see just how much what you learned back then is still influencing what is in your life today.

Each of us grew up steeped in specific cultural circumstances that, along with our parents' relationship, influenced our expectations about what we would have with a man. Our religion, the era we were born in, the country we grew up in, and our family's cultural heritage all contributed to an environment where certain things were acceptable and others were not, where certain things were taken for granted and others were unthinkable.

But whether we grew up in the war-torn 1940s, conservative 1950s, the radical 1960s, the wild 1970s, or the decadent 1980s, we couldn't escape the cultural influences of the increasingly powerful film, magazine, and television industries. We watched movies and sitcoms, pored over women's magazines, and read romance novels—and our expectations about men and relationships were set.

## Love, Hollywood Style

If your fairy godmother had come to you when you were five, she would have whispered in your ear that Disney's versions of *Snow White* (1937), *Cinderella* (1950), and *Sleeping Beauty* (1959) were fantasies. You couldn't possibly be expected to be as good, as beautiful, or as lucky as any of those heroines. She would have added the fact that the Prince in each of these stories is idealized, that no man would *always* measure up to the Prince's manly valor and silent heroism. And finally, she would have informed you that no relationship between a man and a woman could be sustained from two sentences of dialogue, a pretty face, and a kiss.

But because our fairy godmothers failed to show up and enlighten us, we were left to draw our own conclusions. And because the fairy tale was much more compelling than the reality of our parents' marriages, we swallowed it whole. We believed the story of the green water to such an extent that as adults we are still rejecting the clear water because it just looks wrong to us.

Take the example of Snow White, a woman who lived with seven men who adored her and would do anything for her. (Not only that, but also they were willing to share her among all seven of them!) The problem is that they were short, funny looking and had weird names—so she didn't even consider them as potential mates. The only one who could save her from her poisoned sleep, the only one she could fall in love with, was Prince Charming, who didn't do anything except lift her onto his horse and ride away with her. He was not the one who worked all day and brought flowers to her glass coffin every evening. But he had to be the right one because he *looked* like the right one.

*Snow White* taught us that the good men are nerdy and the handsome ones are only around once in a while. We have to wait for them and be grateful when they show up. Our Prince must be gallant and handsome, and because there is only one Prince, we are always searching for him. Meanwhile we ignore all the good men who would do anything to make us happy.

Plenty of movies reinforce this dichotomy between the available men who look nerdy because they are so eager, and the unavailable ones who look desirable because they are so nonchalant. If you've seen *Pillow Talk* (1959), remember Doris Day pining after Rock Hudson, who swears he'll never marry? She pushes away Tony Randall, who will do anything for her and who begs her to marry him. *Gone with the Wind* (1939) may be the greatest example of this syndrome. Scarlett O'Hara's love triangle exemplifies the classic dilemma of the American woman, especially as popularized by Hollywood: she loves the man who doesn't love her and can't love the man who does.

Whatever the medium, the culture we grew up in was addicted to romance. And romance meant drama. It meant that love between a man and a woman was the one thing no one could live without. And almost always, it meant that a woman's life would center around a man's. A woman was incomplete without a man. She needed a man to save her, make her happy, disappoint her, and marry her.

We think it's romantic when two people can't be together, when they misunderstand each other, and when heartbreak happens. Didn't you cry when you watched *The Way We Were* (1973) and *Ghost* (1990)? A real story of a good relationship would be pretty boring, wouldn't it? The heroine would come home and nestle on the sofa with her husband, and maybe he would rub her shoulders. They would talk about their day a little, and then watch the news on TV. They might order pizza or heat up leftovers and talk about what to do for the weekend. After a while they would floss, brush their teeth, go to bed, and cuddle. Not exactly the stuff soap operas are made of. *Days of Our Lives* wouldn't last a week if it showed only happily married couples.

> ✍♥
>
> **We ignore all the good men who would do anything to make us happy.**
>
> ✍♥

Scarlett O'Hara pining after the man who can't love her and dismissing the man who does; Audrey Hepburn in *My Fair Lady* transforming into a Princess; *The Honeymooners* digging at each other constantly; Nancy Drew never needing a boy to help her on her quest; Katherine Hepburn's characters swinging between career and husband. Whatever the media, you were presented with ideals to live up to and scripts for how to live. Just because you're grown up now doesn't mean you aren't still measuring men against that ideal and trying to live by that script. Movies and TV shows like the following influenced us then and still influence us now:

Disney's fairy tales
*Casablanca* (1942)
*West Side Story* (1961)
*My Fair Lady* (1964)
*The Sound of Music* (1965)
*Grease* (1978)
*An Officer and a Gentleman* (1982)
*Pretty Woman* (1990)
*Sixteen Candles* (1984)

*My Three Sons* (1960–1972)
*The Brady Bunch* (1969–1974)
*The Mary Tyler Moore Show*
  (1970–1977)
*The Love Boat* (1977–1986)
*Dallas* (1978–1991)
*The Cosby Show* (1984–1992)
*Moonlighting* (1985–1989)
*Sex in the City* (1998–   )

But how could any man live up to Cary Grant, Humphrey Bogart, Sean Connery, Harrison Ford, or Tom Cruise? How could any relationship survive the expectation of happily ever after? Of course, today there are a few good movies out there that go against Hollywood stereotypes—*Crossing Delancey, Ever After, Baby Boom, Enchanted April,* to name a few—but they weren't around when we were children. And there are still plenty of unrealistic movies out there today—movies that can cause us to cast a critical eye on our men.

Rachel had been happily married for ten years when she took her husband to see *Pretty Woman.* She adored her husband and was happily married. But after the movie, she started an argument with him. At first she didn't know why she was so angry, but suddenly she realized it was because she was measuring her husband against Richard Gere's character, a modern version of the Prince. And of course her husband was coming up short. "And I have a good relationship with my husband," Rachel mused. "I wonder what kind of damage this movie is doing to women who *don't* have good relationships."

What were the movies and television shows that you adored, that perhaps you watched again and again? See if you can begin to notice how they influenced you, and what they taught you.

## Tears on Your Pillow: The Influence of Popular Songs

The songs we used to listen to—and still do—also contribute to our expectations about relationships. In fact they often have an almost subliminal effect on our outlook—and most popular songs just reinforce the heartache, the difficulty, and the ideals of romantic love. Think about how you feel even today when you hear the songs you listened to as a kid:

| | |
|---|---|
| "The Man That Got Away" | "Somewhere Out There" |
| "A Good Man Is Hard to Find" | "Tears on My Pillow" |
| "Chances Are" | "It's My Party" |
| "You Are My Destiny" | "Silhouettes on the Shade" |
| "Heartbreak Hotel" | "Memories" |
| "Stairway to Heaven" | "Come Sail Away" |

"Heaven"                              "Leaving on a Jet Plane"
"Islands in the Stream"               "Lady in Red"
"I Will Always Love You"              "Total Eclipse of the Heart"
        "You're Nobody Till Somebody Loves You"

Some women think they weren't affected. Not so. One of the women at Life Works is a women's studies professor who has written several feminist books—and her hobby is singing torch songs. Think back to the songs you listened to when you were growing up. What songs tugged at your heartstrings and what did they teach you about what it meant to love a man?

## Even Feminists Want Their Princes!

Perhaps you're thinking that the women's movement swept away a lot of the old stereotypes. Well of course it did, but what did we get in their place? We have a forum for seeing that the old model for romantic relationship doesn't work—but we don't necessarily have a new model that *does*. With nothing new to replace it, the old, romantic ideal persists, despite all the gains of feminism. Okay, perhaps we no longer need men to make our lives complete. So what *do* we need them for? We don't really know, do we? In fact even many women who were active feminists in the 1960s and 1970s *still* find themselves longing for a Prince.

Face it. Whether you lived through the women's movement or your mother did, your expectations about relationship are still shaped by the old model. And to the degree that you are still expecting the fairy tale, you will not be able to know what would really satisfy you in a relationship.

## Examining Your Own Expectations

A good way to start thinking about your ideals and expectations is to rent some of the movies you remember watching in your childhood. Seeing them from a new perspective will give you insight into the ideas you formed about men, relationship, and how to be a woman in the world. When you look at the movies now, try to remember the little girl you were. What would you have concluded from watching those movies?

It would also be good to examine what you have been watching, listening to, and reading as an adult. *Sex and the City* is a modern exploration of relationship, yet each woman is still comparing her life to traditional cultural expectations. Movies such as *Message in a Bottle, The Bridges of Madison County, Only You, Sleepless in Seattle, Kate & Leopold,* and *Moulin Rouge* might leave you feeling like your life is coming up short in the romance department. Many "women's interest" books are little more than up-to-date romance novels. Women's magazines are constantly giving advice on how to find, feed, and keep a Prince—and how to decorate a castle. We are still being saturated with information about how life should be, and that information is still mostly incorrect. We are still being told that water is green, and we are still searching for the green water.

Once you stop waiting for the Prince, you will be able to start seeing that there are desirable men out there who are also sweet. They are the ones you haven't been noticing until now because that category doesn't exist in the *Snow White* version of life. Only when you can begin to explore the influences that have you waiting for a Prince will you be able to begin having what you want with a real, live, perfectly imperfect, caring, wonderful man—a man whom you can find attractive *and* who will treat you well. He does exist. He is waiting for you to recognize him.

*Your mother never told you. . .*
  *how much movies, books, television, magazines,*
  *and songs would influence you.*

## Enter Mom and Dad

Jillian tapped her black pen against her teeth thoughtfully, then wrote, *"Never realized how much movies, TV, etc., influenced me. Can't believe I never noticed, especially as I think of myself as an aware, intelligent woman ... I guess it's so ingrained I just didn't see it."*

Jillian put down her pen as Marilyn began to talk again.

❧

**If you want to know what you expect, look at what you have.**

❧

"Now that we've explored the cultural influences you grew up with, each of you is going to have a chance to look at your own personal history," said Marilyn. "You'll be focusing on how your parents, or the adults who raised you, formed what you expect in relationships. Remember that what you expect is what you get. In fact, if you want to know what you expect, look at what you have. If you don't have the relationship you want, you learned something from your parents that makes you believe you can't have it."

Jillian picked up her pen in a hurry. *"Yikes, my parents!"* she scribbled. *"Do I really expect to get what they had with each other? Explains a lot."*

"I'll start by telling you the story of Cathy," Marilyn said. "Cathy worked for the State Department. She loved her job, especially because she spent much of her time traveling. She had worked hard to achieve her professional goals and she was stimulated by her hectic schedule and frequent travels. Yet she wasn't totally happy without a man to share her life.

"Cathy didn't think she could ever get married. Who would put up with her long periods away from home and the unpredictable nature of her schedule? She resigned herself to being a single career woman.

"Sound familiar?" Marilyn suggested. "I bet many of you think you can never get married because you have some flaw a man could never put up with.

"On the urging of a friend, Cathy signed up for this Workshop," Marilyn continued. "She didn't have high hopes because she thought the weekend would be tailored toward women who had more traditional jobs—and who were willing to give up their careers when they met the right man. Mentally she took herself out of the running, but she forced herself to listen and to participate in the exercises."

Marilyn put on her reading glasses. "Now I'm going to read to you from a letter Cathy wrote to all of us at Life Works a few years after taking the Workshop," she said. "She gave me permission to share it with you.

"'It had never occurred to me that I could have what I wanted,' Cathy wrote. 'My parents had a traditional marriage where my dad worked and my mom stayed home. I thought that being a wife meant having to be home to care for the house and kids. It didn't help that my parents were always asking me about my love life and bugging me about getting married. They were proud that I had an interesting job, but they thought of it as something I was doing until I could find a husband.

"'Even though I disagreed with my parents, I felt the pressure to get married. Not only that, but I was lonely and wanted a man in my life. I just couldn't reconcile my work life with having a man. I'd seen other women doing it, but it didn't shake my belief that I couldn't have a marriage that fit my hectic schedule. I thought I had to have my parents' marriage, or nothing. It seems so simplistic when I put it that way, but it's really what I believed.

"'The Workshop helped me see that there are as many ways of designing a relationship as there are women. For the first time it occurred to me that most of the men I met on the job were married. They managed to have relationships even though they had the same travel schedule as I did. And if they could have it, maybe I could have it too.'"

Marilyn looked over the top of her glasses at the women in front of her. "I want to point out here that many of you share

Cathy's dilemma. If you think it's surprising that she didn't realize she could have a marriage that was different from her parents', think again. When you look at your own history you will be amazed to see how much you've decided about what you could have is based on what your parents had. It's unavoidable. It's your history and it is still with you."

Jillian realized she'd been biting the tip of her pen. She wrote, *"Look at the relationships I've had—they have all ended badly, just like my parents' marriage did. It's kind of weird but I never really considered that one had to do with the other."*

"When Cathy opened herself to the possibility of marriage, she was surprised to find herself meeting eligible men for the first time," Marilyn went on. "Some men were put off by her schedule, but some didn't seem to mind it at all. After a couple of short-term relationships, she met Nick, a pilot. Here's what she wrote us about Nick:

"'Nick traveled just as much, or more, than I did. He loved that I flew all over the world. We could compare stories of all the places we'd been, and we both understood how it was to be away from home so much. When he proposed, I couldn't believe it. I was afraid we'd never see each other, but we made an effort to co-ordinate our schedules.

"'Since we're both people who enjoy our careers, we are perfectly happy to have one or two weeks out of the month together. That way, when we're apart we can concentrate totally on work— and when we're together we appreciate each other fully. The fun part is, we get to choose where we'll spend our time together. Though we have a house in Washington, we don't spend much time there. We meet in exotic places like Taiwan and Greece, and our lives together are like one big vacation! I am happier than I ever dreamed I could be, and my marriage is very different from my parents'. This may never have happened if I hadn't explored my history.'"

Marilyn looked up. "What Cathy discovered was that she

could have a marriage that was very different from her parents'. She had expected not to be able to have a marriage if she wanted to keep her career, so in order to have what she wanted she had to change her expectation. Freeing herself from her expectation of what a marriage would be allowed her to use her creativity to design a marriage that worked for her. It's a great example of how we limit what we allow ourselves to have based on our history— and how exploring our history can free us to have what we want."

"*Maybe I could have a better marriage than my parents*," Jillian wrote. "*Strange that I've never thought of that before. Look into my history and see how my parents' marriage formed my expectations about relationship. Could I really learn to expect something different—and have it?*"

## Your mother never told you. . .
*that what you expect is what you get.*

### History Repeats Itself

While American culture was showing you unrealistic, ideal relationships, your parents were living through real-life issues, crises, arguments, and disappointments. Their relationship was your personal laboratory, showing you up close what you could expect from life. It probably looked pretty different from the Hollywood or sitcom model, and given a choice you would probably select the Hollywood version every time. Yet growing up in your particular family meant you were absorbing its behavior every moment. You didn't have other role models that were consistently around in such an intimate setting, and you needed to figure life out from something.

Imagine being a child and having to make sense of the constant barrage of experiences, expectations, praise, blame, feelings, and thoughts that were coming at you all day, seven days a week. Life was very stimulating and confusing because it was all happening so fast—and most of it was happening for the first time.

Knowing what to expect became very important, because if you knew what to expect you would know how to behave. Yet there wasn't time to sit down and figure out what would work in each moment as it happened—so you watched your parents, your older siblings, your extended family, and your peers for clues. And for the most part you just copied what they did so you could relax and feel confident that you could negotiate life.

## Like Mother/Father, Like Daughter

Your parents were your role models for how to act in a relationship. Their marriage taught you what you could expect from a relationship, and how your mother reacted to your father showed you what to expect from men. A lot of what you learned was probably quite positive and helpful. Unfortunately, though, some things you learned in the laboratory provided by your parents ended up hurting you when you started having relationships of your own.

We all do what our parents did. We can't help following what we were taught. Our expectations of how relationships will be, what men are like, and what women are like were *all* born and raised in our families, just like we were. And what we expect is what we get. If we expect men to be wimps, we get wimpy men. If we expect relationships to be difficult, we get difficult relationships. If we expect that it's hard to get attention from a man, we'll have trouble getting attention.

We all relive our childhood experiences over and over again in adulthood—even when we're trying not to. Rebelling against what our parents taught us is often just doing the opposite of what we saw them do. But only doing what they did or the opposite of what they did limits us greatly. When we realize that everything we've been doing is in response to what we learned as children, we can begin to see that there might be other choices we've never thought of before.

## Sharon

Sharon was always attracted to men with red hair. Her first crush in sixth grade had red hair, her first "steady" boyfriend in ninth grade had red hair, and the first man who proposed to her in college had red hair. At a party she would always gravitate toward a redhead, no matter what his personality was like. Bad boy, nerd, athlete, or intellectual—she was at his side immediately, adoring him. When he didn't end up being ambitious, worldly, and devoted to her, Sharon felt hurt and surprised.

*What has been the same about all the important relationships you've had?*

Somehow Sharon managed to miss her attraction to redheads when she examined why she hadn't yet had a successful long-term relationship with a man. "I guess there just aren't any good men left," she said at the Workshop. "I waited too long, and now I'll just have to resign myself to being single."

That weekend, Sharon began to pay real attention to her history. A light bulb went on for her when she had to answer the question, "What has been the same about all the important relationships you've had?" She realized that she hadn't been choosing men based on the fact that they liked her, wanted a commitment, worked hard, had a good sense of humor, or any of the other qualities she really wanted in a spouse. For thirty years she had been choosing men based on a single physical trait—without knowing it!

As she delved into her history, Sharon recalled that her father's older brother had a full head of red hair. Her father adored his brother and always sought him out at family gatherings. The two men had a special relationship and Sharon's father positively glowed when his brother paid attention to him. "He's a real man," her father would say after seeing his brother. "Smart, clear about what he wants, and a go-getter...there aren't many out there like him."

Sharon realized she'd taken on her father's adoration by choosing redheaded men. Their hair color represented ambition, success, and the ability to take care of her financially. In short, a redheaded man was a Prince. Recognizing that she was choosing men based on her historical expectation allowed Sharon to start considering men who were actually steady, loyal, and generous rather than men whose hair color was their only qualification as a potential mate. She could now choose from a list of attributes longer than only "red hair"!

It's hard to believe that Sharon didn't notice her pattern for thirty years. Yet we all have patterns based on our history that are easy for others to see and may be difficult for us to see. Even being attracted to a certain physical feature, as Sharon was, can be based on something historical. Patterns are so woven into the fabric of who we are that we don't notice them. Just as we don't see our own face unless we look in the mirror, we don't see our patterns unless we carefully examine our history. Sometimes the parallels with our history are as blatant as Sharon's, and sometimes they're subtler.

**There are people and circumstances in your life today that parallel people and circumstances from your history.**

It's easier to see how others are repeating their history than to see it in your own life. Take a look at some of your friends' or relatives' relationships and you will see they live their lives based on what they learned in their families. And it is true for you too. It may be difficult to see at first, but there are people and circumstances in your life today that parallel people and circumstances from your history.

### Janet

Janet's father worked the graveyard shift at the local canning factory. He worked from midnight until eight o'clock in the morning, then came home and ate dinner as the rest of the family was having breakfast. He was always very tired when he came home and didn't want a lot of chatter around the table. Sometimes Janet's mother would try to have a conversation, but she would give up after a while when she realized he would only answer her in grunts. He preferred to eat silently, and then go into the living room and watch television for a while. While he was slumped in front of the TV, Janet's mother would often go in and try to talk to him. "Can't it wait till later, Madge?" he'd say in annoyed voice.

"Well, no, Fred," Janet's mother would say, her voice rising. "I realize you're tired, but we have kids and a home to attend to. You don't seem very interested in us, but in case you care, the lawn needs mowing and you know I'm not strong enough to push the mower around."

"Fine, fine, I'll do it. Just let me get some rest first," her father would say, waving Madge away with a flick of his hand.

"But it's *not* fine!" Madge would move so she was standing in front of the television with her arms crossed. "Janet has to go to the dentist tomorrow and I don't know how we'll pay for it. Jason lost his baseball glove and says he needs a new one. The toilet is leaking and I want to know if you can fix it or if we need to call a plumber, and it's been so long since you've done anything around here—"

"For Pete's sake, Madge!" Janet's father would explode. "Would you stop nagging me? Every day it's the same thing, nag, nag, nag. It's a wonder I come home at all." And he would turn off the TV and go into their bedroom, slamming the door. Her mother would set her jaw firmly and go back into the kitchen to clean up after the meal.

Witnessing her parents' interactions day in and day out for the whole of her childhood, Janet learned that:

*Men are distant*
*Men aren't interested in women's concerns*

*Janet would have to try very hard to get men's attention*
*Any attention she received would be negative*
*She would have to bear it with a stiff upper lip*

Like all of us, Janet was destined to live out the modeling her parents provided her. Unless she was a very conscious person, she would unthinkingly repeat what her parents had done. As an adult, she would:

*Choose men who were emotionally unavailable*
*Be hurt that they weren't interested enough in her*
*Start nagging them about why they weren't paying attention to her*
*Annoy them to the point where they blew up at her*
*Put up with it because she didn't know it could be any different.*

Alternately, as a teenager Janet might have become aware that there are other ways of doing things, and she might have grown to hate how her parents interacted. She might have taken a vow never to have a relationship like her parents' and never to act like her mother. If she had taken that vow, she would have spent her life in rebellion, doing the opposite of what she saw growing up. As an adult she might do the following:

*Choose men who were overly possessive*
*Be flattered that they took such an interest in her*
*Become gradually aware that their interest was unhealthy*
*Be unable to stand up for herself because she'd taken a vow not to nag*
*Put up with someone because she didn't know what else to do*

Regardless of whether Janet lived out her parents' model or rebelled against it, the result would likely be similar: Unless she managed to find some different role models, she could easily end up in an unhappy relationship because that was all she knew. Yet Janet's future can be different. If, like you, she is willing to take a look at her history and notice how she is repeating what she learned in childhood, she will get a glimmer of awareness that there are different choices out there. She will start to see that she's been limiting herself to two choices: having a man like her father, or having the opposite, or being like her mother, or being the opposite. And she will be able to see that she in fact has a far wider range of choices.

*Your mother never told you. . .*
*that you would repeat what your parents*
*taught you, even when you're trying not to.*

## With Awareness Comes Power

Once you see how you've been acting from what happened in your history, you can choose to work against this pattern and have your life be different from your parents' lives. Yet even when you're aware, you need to stay on your toes and notice what you're doing. If you're not awake, you may end up being just like your parents without realizing it.

### Diana

Diana's mother was the undisputed leader of her circle of friends. In private some of them called her "The General," but they would never dare say it to her face. At home, she lorded over her husband, too. She looked down on him as unworthy of her, and it seemed like whatever he did wasn't good enough. Diana hated how critical and demanding her mother was, and how she browbeat Diana's father into submission. Diana's father adored her mother and would always give in to her, even when her demands were unreasonable.

Diana sympathized with her father. "I'll never be like my mother," she vowed. "I will treat a man better than my dad is treated."

Diana married a man whom she knew would never be submissive. She was determined not to have a browbeaten husband. She made a great effort to be soft spoken, give in to her husband's desires, and never criticize him. When he said, "Diana, why can't you ever put the dishes away in the right place?" or "Why do you always burn the toast?" she would take a deep breath, apologize, and promise to do it better. After three years, however, Diana realized that the more she was soft spoken and giving in, the more he accused her, criticized her, and nagged her. When his behavior escalated to the point of abuse, she finally left.

Diana's divorce was hard on her, and to help herself she started seeing Sylvia, a Guidess at Life Works. She explored her history and looked at the reasons she might have had such a troubled relationship. One day Diana remembered the vow she'd taken as a teenager.

"I vowed never to be domineering like my mother," she gasped. "And instead, I married a man just like her!"

"It sure sounds that way," said Sylvia. "That's a great insight. So if you weren't your mother in your marriage, who were you?"

Diana's eyes widened. "I guess because I vowed never to be like Mom, I went in the opposite direction—and became my father!"

Sylvia nodded. "And like your father, you didn't stand up to your spouse."

"No, and I accepted the ever-increasing abuse—just as my father submitted to my mother.

"Well, next time I marry I will *not* become my father again," Diana vowed.

A few months later, Diana met a sweet, yet strong and loving man. They were married a year after they met. Diana was sure that by finding a man who was gentle *and* strong she would break the pattern of her parents' relationship. Yet after a couple of years, she and her husband began having serious problems. Diana found many things wrong with him and grew more and more impatient with his faults, and before long she was beginning to nag and criticize him. She couldn't seem to let him alone, and she was sure he was all wrong for her.

One morning Diana called Sylvia to set up an appointment after a particularly difficult argument with her husband.

"Why is it so awful between us?" she sobbed.

"It sounds like something historical," said Sylvia. "Can you think of a historical reason you're so dissatisfied with your husband—a reason that may have nothing to do with him and everything to do with your past?"

Realization hit Diana like a thunderbolt.

"I can't believe it," she said. "I mean, he isn't perfect or anything but this really *doesn't* have anything to do with him. Because I vowed not to be like my father this time, I actually came full circle and became the one I *never* wanted to be—my mother."

Why did Diana's behavior swing between the two extremes of her father and her mother? Because her family's history taught her that there were only two ways of behaving in a relationship: abuser or abused. Even though she observed different behavior in her friends' families, it was impossible for her to be any other way than how she was trained to be in her own family until she woke up to the pattern. That is how strongly our history can affect what we have in our lives today.

> We attract people and situations that cause us to repeat our past—until we become aware of our patterns and can change our expectations.

When history is repeating itself, it often goes unnoticed. If we do notice a pattern, we tend to chalk it up to coincidence. Yet *it is not a coincidence* when we end up dating a man who yells like our mother did or marrying a man who ignores us like our father did. We treat others the way we were treated in childhood, and we expect to be treated that way too. Since that is what we expect, it is what we get. It's that simple. We attract people and situations that cause us to repeat our past—until we become aware of our patterns and can change our expectations.

*Your mother never told you . . .*
*that your family taught you what to expect*
*from a man and how to be with a man.*

## We Get Exactly What We Expect

Jillian's notebook was filling up with insights from the first few hours of the Workshop. She had done several exercises to delve into her own history and she felt like the new information was already changing the way she looked at her life.

*"No wonder I keep attracting men who resemble Dad in so many ways,"* she wrote during a break. *"Thought it was a coincidence . . . liked men with a good sense of humor but never apologize, men who made promises and wanted to keep them but somehow couldn't—but it's not. Expecting men to act like him so that's what I find. Keep having the same problems with them over and over. Now that I know this, something else can happen. Wow!"*

Marilyn came in from the break and sat down. The room gradually quieted.

"Here we are again," Marilyn said with a smile. "So—your past has *everything* to do with your present. We all know that now, right?"

A chorus of "Yes," "Absolutely," and "Right" resounded through the room.

"And knowing this gives you the ability to change the present if you want to, right?"

Nods all around.

"So it is really important to remember that you get what you expect," said Marilyn emphatically. "Let me say it again:

**You get what you expect.**

"And when you know that, you have the power to have something different. How can you have something different? *By changing what you expect.*

"Expectations are learned, and anything that's learned can be unlearned and replaced with new information. Once you know that you have what you expect, things will begin to shift. Awareness is ninety percent of the cure. When you are aware, you will be able to be awake in the moment and *notice.* You can notice *when* something is historical, notice *what* you are expecting, and notice *why* you might be making the choices you're making."

> Expectations are learned, and anything that's learned can be unlearned and replaced with new information.

"*My expectations,*" wrote Jillian in a red scrawl, and then below it she made a list.

1) *Never find the right man and have to settle like mother.*
2) *Have to be long-suffering like mother and stay while marriage goes down the tubes.*
3) *Marriage will go sour like theirs. How depressing! No wonder I'm not married.*

"We all have things we need to understand about what we've been expecting based on our cultural history and our family history," Marilyn continued. "It's like tilting your head so you can see your life from a different angle. You get a different perspective that way. Once you can see it differently, you can gain some insight into why you've had the relationships you've had. And that shift in perspective allows you to start expecting something different—so you can have something different.

Jillian scribbled frantically. "*This is cool! Tilt head—change perspective—change perception. Different thoughts lead to different feelings—different feelings to different action. And voila—different outcome! Makes perfect sense, and it all starts with just a small tilt of the head. I can do that.*"

"Now I'd like you to get out a pen and paper," Marilyn said. "I'm going to give you a list of new things you can expect. It would be good to have this in your notebook so you can refer to it later."

"*New things to expect*," Jillian wrote at the top of a fresh page. She copied the list Marilyn was reading aloud:

**There is no Prince.**

**I will have relationships with real, live human males.**

**My relationships don't have to look like my parents' relationship.**

**I can find the man I want.**

**I can create the relationship I want.**

**There are a lot of good men out there.**

**There is nothing wrong with me.**

**There is a man who is looking for a woman just like me.**

"Aren't these great things to expect?" Marilyn asked. "It makes life a lot more enjoyable when you have an optimistic, positive outlook. And you will be amazed at what a difference it makes. As you become aware of your history and awaken to what you expect, you will be tilting your head slightly so you can see your life from a different angle. When you see things differently, you will experience a shift in perception. Changing your perception allows you to have different thoughts. When you have different thoughts, you will have different feelings. Having different feelings will prompt you to take a different action. And when you take a different action, you will produce a different result."

tilt your head → see things differently → shift perspective → different thoughts → different feelings → different action → different result

"When you can see the reason for what you have, you can stop blaming yourself for it," Marilyn continued. "If every man ends up disappointing you, you could know there was nothing wrong with you. Maybe your mother gave you the wrong information about men. Maybe you've been attracting men who disappoint you because that's what you expect—or perhaps you test men in a way that ensures they will disappoint you. Maybe now you can expect something different.

"Knowing you're getting the relationship you expect allows you to have a more optimistic viewpoint when you meet a man who interests you," Marilyn went on. "You can now expect that not all men will disappoint you. You can take some time to learn about a man's past and find out if he's a man who's let down other women or not. And once you're with him, you can stay awake and notice when you're getting what you want."

*"Good point,"* wrote Jillian. *"Easy to focus on the negative, especially with negative expectations. Always looking for ways those negative expectations are being fulfilled—instead of noticing when treated well. Glass is half-empty syndrome. Didn't know any better before. With Ernie, only noticed when he left soda cans everywhere, not when he did the dishes."*

"When he's not disappointing you, you can enjoy what a man has to offer. When you're enjoying him, you'll be more likely to encourage him rather than criticize him. And when he's feeling appreciated, there's a much better chance he will live up to your optimistic expectations."

Marilyn held out her hands, palms up. "Makes sense, right? Do you see how expecting something different allows you to *get* something different? Before you know it, you will have the kind of relationship you've never had before.

"Being aware of your expectations allows you to change," said

Marilyn. "You will be able to break the pattern of your history. You will be able to open the way to having what you want with a man. And you will have the opportunity to be happy!"

*Your mother never told you...*
   *that you have the ability to change what you expect.*

*Think about...*

 **What you expect in a relationship**

*The exercises for Chapter Two can be found on page 262.*

# Chapter Three

## The Beliefs You Formed

Pam's mother was an attractive woman who was afraid of losing the svelte figure she was so proud of. She was constantly worrying about how she looked, stepping onto the scale, and trying the latest weight-loss fads. Pam was a chubby child, much to her mother's dismay. She watched Pam anxiously for signs that she was going to lose her "baby fat." By the time Pam was ten, however, it was obvious that her chubbiness was only increasing. "I'm joining Weight Watchers," her mother said to her one day. "And you're going to do the program along with me."

Pam hated being on a diet and cheated as often as she could get away with it. One day her mother caught her eating a candy bar behind the sofa.

"Oh, Pam, what am I going to do with you?" she said, shaking her head in disappointment.

"What's wrong with the way I am?" Pam asked defiantly.

"Don't you understand?" her mother said. "You'll never find a man if you're fat. You'll end up like your Aunt Mildred, fat and alone at fifty."

Pam rolled her eyes and stomped out of the room. But from then on, her weight became a constant point of attention in their household. Her brother teased her whenever he saw her eating something fattening, her mother weighed her once a week and was always disappointed, and her father joked about Aunt Mildred and the overweight nurses he worked with at the hospital who ate doughnuts every day. Pam continued to put on weight steadily through her adolescence, and she became more and more self-conscious. She had a small group of girlfriends, none of whom ever had dates on Saturday night. They would sit in Pam's bedroom, watching TV, eating chips, and making fun of the girls who mooned over boys all the time. They spent a lot of time honing witty remarks and snappy comebacks, taking comfort in the fact that they were far more intelligent than the popular girls at school. Yet Pam secretly envied the thin, bubbly girls on the cheerleading squad who dated the jocks on the football team.

Pam knew that she could never have a man in her life as long as she was fat. Movies, television, and magazines proved to her that her belief was true. On screen, the woman who got the man was always slender. The few heavy female characters were always the amusing sidekicks who ended up alone. And the glamorous women in fashion magazines were always fabulously skinny. Pam looked in vain for overweight women who were portrayed as attractive.

Pam fantasized about losing forty pounds, entering college as a slim coed, and getting engaged to the captain of the football team. But she could never seem to lose the weight, and she went through college without dating at all. She did very well in her studies, however, and was pleased to land a good job after graduation. She consoled herself with the thought that if she couldn't get a man, she could at least be a successful career woman—something her mother had never been. Yet she was often lonely and longed for male companionship. Since she could never seem to lose that extra forty pounds, though, she resigned herself to being single.

## It Is All in Your Head

In her late twenties Pam became friends with a coworker named Beverly. Beverly was about twenty pounds more overweight than Pam, yet she carried herself with a confidence that Pam envied. She wore bright clothes and red lipstick, had a new hairstyle nearly every month, and freely gave out recommendations about the best new restaurants in town. Pam sought out Beverly's companionship and they started meeting regularly after work for drinks. As their friendship grew, however, Pam discovered that Beverly was never available on the weekends.

Every Thursday when she tried to make plans to get together, she'd hear the same refrain: "Sorry, hon, I'm busy this weekend."

Finally Pam's curiosity got the better of her and she asked Beverly, "Where do you go every weekend?"

"Oh, on Friday night I go out of town to meet my boyfriend, and I spend Saturday with him," Beverly said. "And then on Saturday night I come back to the city to spend time with my *other* boyfriend." She threw her head back and laughed.

"You're joking, right?" Pam asked tentatively. She figured Beverly couldn't be serious. She probably went to visit her mother in the suburbs every weekend.

"It's funny, but I'm not joking," she said. "I'm seeing these two guys at the same time and it's driving both of them crazy! I let them know about each other—subtly, of course—and they're both eaten up with jealousy. Ron, the one I see on Fridays, has even been hinting about marriage lately. Oh, it's so much fun, I tell you."

Pam was speechless. Beverly had not one, but *two* boyfriends? It was impossible that someone even heavier than Pam could have a love life. Didn't everyone know that fat girls couldn't get a man? Yet it was a fact—Beverly had two men who were crazy about her and who were competing for her attention.

Pam went home after her conversation with Beverly and found that she could think of nothing but Beverly's revelation. How could it be possible that she had lived her whole life knowing an overweight girl couldn't get the guy, when hefty Beverly took it for granted that she could have two men vying for her attention? She felt shaken, as if the foundation she'd always rested upon was cracking.

The next afternoon Beverly and Pam sat in a booth at the diner down the street from their office.

"Bev, I have to ask you something."

"Go for it," said Bev.

Pam giggled. "Actually, it's about men. Listen, I have to admit I was shocked when you told me you had two boyfriends. How do you do it?"

"You know, I never thought about it," she admitted. "I've always had boyfriends, even in high school."

"But how did you get like that? I mean, I wouldn't have the confidence to put myself out there like that."

"Hmm. Well, all the women in my family are heavy—and the men were always saying that a woman should have some meat on her bones. They appreciated robust women. So I guess I just took it for granted that there were men who wanted larger women. And I never thought there would be a shortage of them. My grandmother used to say, 'Men are like streetcars—there's always another one coming.' And I believed her, because there always *was* another one."

"So you believed that men would be interested in you, and that there were plenty of them out there," Pam mused.

Pam shook her head in wonder. "So, what I've always taken to be the truth isn't really the *truth*. Amazing. I mean, how could it be the truth when your experience has been so different from mine? They can't *both* be the truth. If I could believe what you believe I could date, I could have a relationship, I could even get married!" She felt a great gust of relief sweep through her. Perhaps she wouldn't have to end up like Aunt Mildred after all. And maybe the reason Aunt Mildred was single was that she didn't want a man—or that she had a different belief that would stop her from being married.

My grandmother used to say, "Men are like streetcars— there's always another one coming."

Like Pam and Beverly, we all have beliefs that limit us and beliefs that empower us. Yet it's the limiting beliefs that we need to be concerned about because they are what keep us from having what we want. When we think a belief is the truth, we attract experiences that bear it out. We create rules for ourselves about what can and cannot happen in our lives.

*Your mother never told you...*
*that you would be limited by your beliefs.*

## How Our Families Shape Our Beliefs

Beverly and Pam each formed different beliefs because they had different childhoods. And like them, you created beliefs based on your response to what you experienced in your history. Your beliefs are different from anyone else's because they stem from your unique reaction to your childhood experiences. Your parents' relationship and your family's interactions gave you information about life that you interpreted in your own way. You may have a sibling who has different beliefs about life than you do, even though you grew up in the same household. That's because she responded differently to your family's influence than you did. You developed a belief system all your own based on what your mother and father told you. You created these beliefs whether your parents spoke silently or out loud, whether you formed them consciously or unconsciously.

> **Your beliefs are different from anyone else's because they stem from your unique reaction to your childhood experiences.**

## Mom

The way your mother communicated to you about men influenced your beliefs profoundly. Her feelings about herself, your father, and their relationship had an enormous impact on your perception of life. Your mother was constantly communicating beliefs to you, both verbally and through her actions or body language. She might have done this in some of the following positive or negative ways:

## Positive

*Greeting him warmly every night.*
*Being gentle with him when he had a bad day.*
*Babying him when he was sick.*
*Receiving his gifts gracefully.*
*Accompanying him graciously to company functions.*
*Expecting him to treat her well.*
*Cooking his favorite meal when he returned from a trip.*
*Tiptoeing past their room when he was sleeping.*
*Proudly introducing him to her friends.*

## Negative

*Complaining about him.*
*Showing you her disappointment or resignation.*
*Fighting with him.*
*Worrying that he was off with another woman.*
*Expecting him to treat her badly.*
*Criticizing him to others.*
*Gossiping about him with her mother.*
*Being "unpleasable."*
*Nagging him.*

Whatever her behavior was around your father, your mother was constantly sending you information. Even if you didn't agree with her, you were forming beliefs based on what she was telling and showing you. Some of the beliefs have helped you in your relationships with men, and many of them have hindered you.

## Jessica

Jessica's mother was fond of telling her the story of how she met her father.

"I worked as a nurse for ten years before I met Sean," she would reminisce. "My mother wanted me to go to nursing school. 'It's a good backup,' she said. Well, I went—but I never wanted to be a nurse, you know."

Jessica had heard the story a hundred times before.

"No, all I ever wanted was to get married and raise a family," her mother would sigh. "But my dad died while I was in nursing school, and then I couldn't back out. I had to help my mother, so I got a job at one of the big hospitals after graduation. I thought, oh well, I'll work for a year or two and then I'll marry one of the doctors."

Jessica would cringe inwardly at the backwardness of her mother's thinking. She couldn't believe how women thought back then. A nurse—really! She wanted to be a surgeon, and nothing was going to stop her.

"Well, somehow ten whole years went by, and by the time I was thirty-one I'd nearly given up hope." Her mother would shake her head and take a sip of her tea. "Then one day I was having lunch in the cafeteria, and when I put my tray down on the table something told me to look up. And there he was, standing across from me with a cup of coffee, just staring at me. He sat across from me and we just started talking. Turns out he was there to visit his mother. And he asked me out to dinner. I couldn't believe my luck."

"And the rest is history," Jessica would finish.

"Yes. And here you are, my lovely daughter. Oh, I can't wait until your wedding day. I can just see it now, you can wear my dress, I'm sure it will fit you by then. You've got the same build I had at your age. And we can have it at Holy Angels Church ..."

"Mom!" Jessica, feeling slightly ill, would be compelled to interrupt at this point. "I'm not getting married. How many times do I have to tell you? I'm going to be a famous surgeon. I won't have time for a husband and kids."

"Oh, you'll change your mind when you meet the right man," her mother would murmur complacently.

"Oh, no I won't," Jessica would vow silently. "I'll never be like her, satisfied with family life. I'm going to do something that matters."

**Belief:** *"Having a man means giving up my dreams."*

**Behavior:** *Jessica stuck to her ambitions and became a surgeon. She worked hard through her twenties and thirties and didn't have time for a personal life.*

**Effect:** *When she turned forty, Jessica realized she missed having someone to share her life with. Yet she was convinced that a man wouldn't be able to put up with her unpredictable schedule and grueling hours. She became depressed, certain that because of the career she'd chosen she was destined to be alone.*

## Vivian

Vivian's mother was an intelligent, cultured, and accomplished woman with the reputation of being the perfect wife, mother, and hostess. She entertained frequently and their house was often filled with friends and family. Yet the moment the guests left she would turn into a different person.

"Oh, George, why on earth did you mention the stock market to the Samsons? You *know* they just lost a bundle and they had to take out a second mortgage on their house. Honestly, can't one evening go by without you sticking your foot in your mouth? How can you be such a social dunce?"

"Sorry, dear," Vivian's father would say meekly. He never contradicted her mother's cutting remarks. Vivian felt badly for her father and tried to tell him to stick up for himself, but he would just shrug and retreat into his pipe and his newspaper. And he would often make mistakes, bumble situations, and conduct himself in a way that seemed to justify his wife's treatment of him.

As Vivian got older, she stopped feeling sorry for him and grew to disdain his wimpy behavior as much as her mother did.

*Belief:* "*Men are stupid and weak.*"

*Behavior:* *Vivian treated men with the same scorn her mother had, expecting that they would mess up.*

*Effect:* *Vivian created an environment around her where no man could be successful.*

She had tended to have disastrous relationships with men who failed at business, dropped out of school, or got into trouble with the law. If she did meet a man who might be worthy, her criticism ended up disempowering him and he would eventually leave.

### Alexandra

Alexandra's mother had a glamorous job in the fashion industry. She commuted to the City every day and sometimes had to go away on business trips. Somehow, though, she always managed to find time to attend Alexandra's school plays and cheer for her at her softball games.

"My, how do you do it, Betty?" the other mothers would often exclaim.

"Oh, Ralph helps me out at home," Alexandra's mother would say. The other mothers would shake their heads in admiration. "If only my husband would do that," they would murmur.

Alexandra was proud of her parents' unusual situation. Since her mother didn't get home until nearly seven o'clock, her father would usually make dinner. He was a good cook and as she got older, he let Alexandra help him in the kitchen. She loved the time they spent together trying out new recipes or baking fat loaves of bread. After dinner, her mother would try to help with the dishes but her father would almost always wave her away.

"Alexandra and I can do it, Betty," he would say. "You've had a hard day in the City."

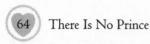

"But you worked all day too," her mother would protest.

"Ah, it's nothing compared to what you do," he would say modestly. And he and Alexandra would have a contest to see who could go faster while they cleaned up the kitchen.

**Belief:** *"Men are happy to help out."*

**Behavior:** *Alexandra grew up expecting that a man would support her in her career and help her out at home.*

**Effect:** *She met men who were willing to pitch in with the housework. She was able to have a good relationship and a successful career.*

*Your mother never told you...*
*that you would create a life in response to her life.*

## Dad

Your beliefs about what men are like are formed to a large extent from your experience with the number one man in your life—Daddy. In childhood you looked to your father for clues to the mysterious beings called *men*. If you want to know what you believe about men, take a good look at your father. He influenced what you believe by:

*If you want to know what you believe about men, take a good look at your father.*

*What he said about women*
*How he interacted with your mother*
*How he treated you*
*The amount of time he spent at home*
*How much or how little he contributed to the housework*
*How much money he made*
*What kinds of demands he made*

Your father's behavior was constantly sending you messages. His behavior taught you how men are, and the way he treated your mother taught you how men interact with women.

## Tory

Tory's father was gone on business trips during much of her childhood. He traveled three weeks out of every month, and when he came home he spent a lot of time sleeping or watching TV because he was exhausted. Tory craved her father's attention, but she wasn't allowed to disturb him when he was sleeping or when he was watching sports on TV. If she tried to get him to notice her he would wave her away. Her father's neglect only made Tory try harder for his attention, even if it meant doing something she knew would get her in trouble.

**Belief:**   *"No man will notice me."*
**Behavior:** *Tory became very promiscuous in high school and college in order to get attention from men.*
**Effect:**   *She never had a relationship that lasted longer than a few weeks.*

## Ellen

Ellen was an "army brat" who grew up constantly moving from one base to another. Her father, an officer, was accustomed to having his orders obeyed at home as well as at work. He had no patience for noise or chaos, and even though the family was always moving he demanded order and organization wherever they were. He insisted they have dinner at exactly six o'clock every evening, that the children would be silent until spoken to at the table, and that the house was always spotless. Ellen's mother complied with all his demands.

Ellen didn't really mind having to eat dinner at the same time every night or go to bed at nine o'clock sharp. What she hated was the nightly inspection. She would have to stand at attention in the middle of her bedroom while her father ran his finger along the windowsill checking for dust, looked in her drawers to make sure her clothes were folded, and checked under the bed to make sure she wasn't hiding anything.

"Vacuum your rug today?" he'd bark.

"Yes, father."

"Finished with all your homework?"

"Yes, father."

"Show me."

Ellen would open her notebooks for his inspection, hoping she hadn't made too many mistakes at her arithmetic. She only hoped he would never think to look between her mattress and box spring where she kept her diary. One day, though, her father surprised her by coming in after lights out. He found her writing in her diary by flashlight under the covers.

"What's this?" he demanded. He seized the little red leather-bound book that she'd bought with her pocket money. "Ah, a diary," he smirked.

"Please, daddy, let me have it back," Ellen begged. But he turned on his heel and marched out of the room, diary in hand. To her humiliation, he read the entire thing out loud to the family the next night at dinner.

"I'll never forgive him," Ellen vowed. And indeed, she grew to increasingly resent his domineering nature and his intrusions into her privacy.

*Belief:* "*Getting close to a man means he will take over my life.*"
*Behavior:* *Ellen put up a lot of walls to protect herself, always maintaining an emotional distance from the men she dated.*
*Effect:* *Since men could only get so close, they would eventually give up.*

## Suzanne

Suzanne's father was a professor at an Ivy League college. He was one of the most popular members of the faculty and was always in demand at parties and functions. Suzanne was proud to be the daughter of such a handsome and charming professor and she loved it when her father invited her to stroll through campus with him. The girls would all giggle and wave to him, and the other professors would stop him to chat.

"Well, hello, Suzanne," they would say. "You really are getting as beautiful as your father says. He brags about you all the time, you know. Apparently you're quite the genius at science too." Suzanne would blush, pleased, and bask in her father's proud gaze.

When her parents gave one of their frequent cocktail parties, Suzanne would often be allowed to help her mother serve drinks and hors d'oeuvres. Then she would watch from a corner as the laughing circle around her father grew more raucous. He was always the center of attention at parties, his dapper clothes and unfailing wit drawing the guests to him like magic. The women in particular flocked around him, throwing their heads back to laugh at his jests and blushing when he smiled at them.

After the party, Suzanne would creep upstairs because she knew what was coming. She would watch from the landing as her mother, tight-lipped, emptied the ashtrays and collected the glasses. Her father would come in from the kitchen and watch her for a while, then say, "What's wrong, Gwen?"

"Oh, nothing," her mother would say.

"Come on, out with it. Is it because that horrid Ellis woman was making eyes at me again?"

"Making eyes at you! She was practically salivating in your martini."

"Now, Gwen, be reasonable. You know she's just like that."

"Well, what about Thelma? You weren't exactly pushing her away when she stood with her ... assets ... practically shoved against you."

Sitting on the landing, Suzanne would listen as the argument continued, then eventually wound down. She always took her father's side in her mind. Could he help it if he was popular? Those women could never have him, anyway. She knew he loved her best.

*Belief:* "Good men are flirtatious."

*Behavior:* When Suzanne started dating she would always go for the man who was surrounded by an admiring group of women. Getting his attention was like a game to her and she felt desired and victorious when he noticed her.

*Effect:* Because she picked men who were flirts, Suzanne found herself constantly in competition with other women. She would grow very jealous of her man's attention and would get so possessive she would end up driving him away.

## Elsa

"Daddy, can I come to work with you today?" Elsa appeared at the breakfast table dressed in her favorite outfit, her hair neatly combed. It was the first day of summer vacation, and she had been looking forward to it all spring. Every time she had a school vacation her father allowed her to visit his architectural firm almost as frequently as she asked.

Elsa's father peeked at her around his newspaper. "Aw, it's just a boring place full of blueprints and dry old geezers," her father teased. He knew how much Elsa loved the high ceilinged, open plan office, and his coworkers who gave her a lot of attention. The female architects in particular would encourage Elsa by praising her drawings and asking her all about school.

"Daddy!" Elsa made a face.

"Oh, okay. But only if you promise to have lunch with me at Henry's Diner."

"Yeah!" Elsa nearly jumped up and down in her excitement. "Will you let me design my own house?"

"Sure," her dad laughed. "But this time, make sure to remember to put in a bathroom. You ended up having to build an outhouse last time."

At the office, Elsa would get her own desk and would spend the day drawing layouts of her own. When she got tired of drawing she would watch the men and women working at their tables, chatting, and consulting with clients in the glassed-in meeting room. She thought it was wonderful that men and women could work together so easily, not like at school where the boys were always picking on the girls. She decided that when she grew up she would have a job just like her father's.

Whatever the situation we came home to every day, we made decisions about how life would be—and our lives have turned out to be a lot like that.

**Belief:** *"Men will respect me."*

**Behavior:** *Elsa became a graphic artist and married an advertising copywriter. After a few years, she and her husband went into business together.*

**Effect:** *They had an equal partnership and respected each other's opinions.*

We all developed beliefs based on the family that raised us—whether or not it was a traditional family unit of mother, father, and children. Aunts and uncles, grandparents, and family friends also had an effect on the beliefs we formed. Whatever the situation we came home to every day, we made decisions about how life would be—and our lives have turned out to be a lot like that.

*Your mother never told you...*
*that how your father was and how he treated*
*you would affect you and your relationships.*

### "That's Life"...Or Is It?

Like Pam, we all live as if certain things are true—and because we think they're true, we never question whether or not something else is possible. "That's just life," we say when the same thing happens to us over and over again. Yet if we look around at our friends' lives, we can see that what happens to us doesn't necessarily happen to them. Why? Because they think something else is true.

How can so many different things be true about life all at once? Because what we think is the truth is actually a *belief we have created about life*. If you want to know what *you* believe, take a look at what you have in your life right now.

**You have what you have in your life because it's what you believe you *can* have.**

If you don't have something that you want, it's likely that you don't believe you can have it. The good news is that, like Pam, becoming aware of what you believe can open up new possibilities for you. When you start noticing that your beliefs aren't necessarily *true*, you can see that other things might be true—and you have the opportunity to have exactly what you want.

Beliefs are deceptive because they look like simple statements about how life is. Some examples of *beliefs* about men and relationships are:

What we think is the truth is actually a *belief we have created about life*. If you want to know what you believe, take a look at what you have in your life right now.

*"Men and women can't get along with each other."*
*"Men and women can't get along without each other."*
*"There are no good available men out there."*
*"There are good available men, but not for a woman like me."*
*"All marriages end badly."*
*"Marriage is a lifelong prison."*
*"Men are untrustworthy."*
*"Trustworthy men are boring."*
*"All men will end up disappointing me."*
*"All men will end up disappointed in me."*
*"He'll always choose someone else instead of me."*
*"He'll choose me and I'll be trapped."*

*"I'm not thin enough / blonde enough / tall enough / witty enough / smart enough / attractive enough / sweet enough / good enough to have the relationship I want with a man."*

*"No man will want to marry a woman who doesn't want children."*

*"No man will want to marry a woman who already has children."*

*"I'm too young to get married."*

*"I'm too old to get married."*

*"Everyone else knows something I don't know."*

*"I know something no one else knows."*

*"Men can't commit."*

*"Men won't commit."*

*"Men want to own me and I need to be free."*

*"All men cheat on their wives."*

*"I'm afraid I can't be faithful to one man for a lifetime."*

*"I can't get too close because he'll end up hurting me."*

*"I can't get too close or I'll end up hurting him."*

*"I'll never have what I want with just one man."*

*"I'll never have what I want with a man."*

It's no accident that we have the beliefs we have. We each formed our beliefs in childhood to help us survive in a complicated world. Life happened very fast when we were small, and we didn't always understand what was going on. Without realizing it, we were constantly making decisions based on what was happening around us in our families, our peer group, and the popular culture. (Oona didn't buy the clear water because she had been taught that water was green, and Pam decided that men wouldn't look at her twice because her mother worried so much about her weight.) These decisions became our beliefs. Our beliefs helped us feel safe because they let us know what we could expect from life, both at that moment and in the future. And we

> **We each formed our beliefs in childhood to help us survive in a complicated world.**

are still living our lives based on those beliefs that were formed before we knew much about ourselves or the world.

*Your mother never told you. . .*
   *that your beliefs create what you have.*

## How the Culture Shapes Our Beliefs

In the last chapter we looked at how the culture affected our *expectations* for relationships. Somewhere along the line, these expectations harden into beliefs. They get mistaken for truth. Of course, no two people will form the same beliefs, even if they were fed the same steady diet of movies and television shows, books, ads, and songs, but the beliefs we form always limit our perceptions of what we can have with a man. Here are a few examples of how the culture's "scripts" for how things should be are translated into self-limiting beliefs.

Eve's mother read fairy tales to her every night before bed. *Cinderella* was her mother's favorite and she read it often. Yet Eve felt very uncomfortable every time her mother read it to her. She would listen to her mother's voice thinking over and over, "I'll never be that good. I can never be that good." And since only good girls got the Prince, Eve knew she would never be able to have one. In order to avoid later disappointment she created the belief, "I don't deserve a Prince." As an adult, Eve lived out her belief by consistently choosing men who were the opposite of princely. The men in her life always treated her badly, took her for granted, and ended up breaking her heart.

Maria's favorite movie star was Greer Garson, and she watched her movies over and over again. Greer Garson always played a strong woman who was capable and efficient. The men in her life looked to her to be the one to shoulder the burden and get done what needed to get done. Maria wanted to be just like Greer Garson. She created the belief, "I have to be strong and capable to have a man love me." Though this belief kept her feeling in control of her life, it also kept her attracting men who were weaker than she was. She would eventually end up resenting them because she had to do all the work.

When she turned eleven, Samantha started reading romance novels and couldn't stop. She read every Harlequin novel she could get her hands on, and later she read fat juicy bestsellers by Jackie Collins and Judith Krantz. She loved reading these books because the drama and glamour transported her from the tension of her parents fighting in her house. She knew she didn't want the lives her parents had. She wanted romance, a man to sweep her off her feet, and adventure. The heroines in the novels always had men ready to swoop in and save them. Samantha decided she would meet a man who would rescue her from her humdrum life. She created the belief, "A man will rescue me." This belief kept Samantha feeling powerless. She attracted men who wanted to dominate and control her.

Wanda watched *The Love Boat* on television every week during her childhood and adolescence. She adored the way the arguments and misunderstandings between each couple would always work out by the end of the hour. At her house, the arguments would go on and on and never seem to be resolved. Watching the couples smooth out their difficulties on the cruise ship gave Wanda a respite from her parents' quarreling. She saw that there was a different way to handle arguments than her parents' constant bickering, and she created the belief, "Arguments can be solved." When she began having relationships with men, she made an effort to listen to their side of an argument and get her point across calmly. Her belief helped her know how to handle it when someone disagreed with her.

What you did with these ideals and scripts was entirely individual to you. If you watched *Carousel* with your friend, you both saw the girl staying with her man even though he hit her. Yet you each formed different beliefs about life after watching it. You may have thought life was romantic and created the belief, "Men who act badly have hearts of gold." Your friend might have been disgusted and created the belief, "All men are selfish and heartless." In living out these beliefs, you would be attracted to bad boys and addicted to reforming them, and she would keep all men at a distance.

Whatever the cultural ideal, we formed a lot of beliefs around it:

| Cultural message | Belief |
|---|---|
| "Blondes have more fun." | "He'll choose the blonde." |
| "Nice girls finish last." | "It's a competition." |
| "There's something wrong if you don't want children." | "Every woman should have a child." |
| "You're nobody 'til somebody loves you." | "Love will make my life worthwhile." |
| "Men need to sow their wild oats." | "A man can't commit to just one woman." |
| "A serious career woman would never give up her job to have a family | "I need to wait to get married." |
| "The course of true love never did run smooth." | "If it's too easy, there's something wrong." |
| "A real man never shows he cares." | "If he's nice to me he must be a nerd." |
| "Women need men but men don't need women." | "I'm more interested in them than they are in me." |
| "A woman's place is in the home." | "I can't have a career and a relationship." |
| "Women can have it all." | "I need to be Superwoman." |
| "Unmarried women are old maids." | "If I'm not married by thirty it's too late." |
| "Men don't want commitment." | "Women want commitment." |
| "Men seldom make passes at girls who wear glasses." | "I'm not attractive enough." |

# Decisions, Decisions

Miranda fell in love for the first time when she was three years old. A year before, her mother had begun telling her she'd get married someday. "When you get married, you'll want to keep a neat house for your husband," she'd explain as she helped Miranda put away her toys. "When you get married, you'll understand why we fight," she'd tell Miranda when her arguments with Miranda's father made Miranda upset. So when she fell in love with Andrew, her mother's cousin, Miranda knew she would marry him. It didn't bother her that Andrew was thirty-three years old—she loved him passionately. Whenever he came to visit, Miranda would peer at him from behind her mother's legs, overcome with emotion. Andrew would tease her until she emerged, then play with her all afternoon. He would swing her around, put her on his shoulders, and dance around the house with her standing on his feet. His visits were the highlight of Miranda's young life.

One day when Miranda was four, her mother dressed her in a new dress and told her they were going to a party. They arrived at church and sat in a pew, Miranda following along and not very curious about what was happening since it was obviously just another boring adult event. Suddenly, the minister said, "We welcome you this afternoon to witness the marriage of Rita and Andrew!" Miranda was devastated. How could Andrew be marrying someone else when she loved him so much? *He had left her for another woman.*

Thirty-five years later Miranda's second husband left her for another woman—just as her first husband had done.

"I can't believe this has happened to me again," she moaned to Miriam, her Guidess. "Are all men just incapable of being faithful?"

"Well, let's see," said Miriam. "How many of your friends are involved with unfaithful men?"

Miranda went through a mental checklist of her friends and was surprised to realize that most of them had been happily married for years. "I can't think of any of my friends whose husbands have cheated on them," she admitted.

"So it's not men," Miriam said. "What else could it be? What's the common denominator in all your relationships?"

Miranda hesitated. "All the men I've been involved with seem really different from each other, but they all end up leaving me for another woman. So I guess the only common denominator is . . . *me*."

Miriam nodded.

"Wow. If it's me, there must be something about me that is drawing these men who cheat into my life," Miranda said.

"Yes. You must have a belief that makes you attract unfaithful ones," said Miriam. "Why don't you think about your childhood this week and see if you can discover a circumstance or an event that influenced you about men."

Miranda woke up three days later with a vivid picture of Andrew's wedding in her mind. She could recall all the details perfectly, including the overwhelming devastation she had felt when she saw Andrew walking down the aisle with his bride. Suddenly she realized that her early experience of abandonment had been incredibly influential in her life. As a four-year-old, she hadn't known how to deal with the feelings of grief and humiliation that overtook her. She didn't have a fairy godmother to say, "It's not that he doesn't love you, it's just that he is thirty years older than you—and your cousin—and you won't be able to marry for many years to come. Andrew chose someone in his appropriate age group to marry, and when you are grown up you will find someone to marry too. Of course you feel bad right now. It's okay to cry, and crying will help you feel better." Instead, at four Miranda had to make a decision that would help her cope with the situation and ensure that she would never feel that badly again.

Miranda shared her realization with her Guidess the following week. "I realized that at that devastating moment I unconsciously formed the belief, 'All men will leave with another woman.' I was trying to protect myself from ever feeling disappointed again. But

The Beliefs You Formed

of course it didn't work. Believing that men will leave me means they always do, and it's devastating every time."

Miranda sighed. "It's actually great to know that I have something to do with what's been happening, because now I can do something about it!"

## But the Psychological Is Not Logical

Like Miranda, when things got too intense or confusing in your childhood you made psychological decisions about what to expect from your life. Then, these decisions turned into beliefs. In moments of trauma, you had to make split-second choices—not only to make sense of the current situation, but to help you know what to expect in the future so you wouldn't ever feel that way again. If Miranda *expected* that any man she fell in love with would leave for another woman, her subconscious reasoned it wouldn't hurt as much whenever one left.

The problem is that this psychological reasoning doesn't work, because the psychological is not logical. Logic would have you see that you never feel less disappointed simply because you expect the worst. When something traumatic happens you are still hurt, even if you were expecting it. Your childhood decision was useful at the time because it helped you tolerate overwhelming feelings. What you couldn't have realized was that the decision you made would become a belief you would live by.

> **When something traumatic happens you are still hurt, even if you were expecting it.**

Though your beliefs might be causing you pain, you may still have some resistance to shifting them. Your beliefs keep you feeling safe. You can predict how things will be. It is human nature to prefer the expected to the unexpected, even if what you expect is something bad. When your expectations are fulfilled you can say, "Aha! I knew that was going to happen, and it happened. I have life all figured out, and all is right with the world." It may be strange to think that you would rather have something bad happen simply because you expect it, than to have something good happen that would challenge your beliefs about how life is. Yet it is human nature to prefer to be right about something, and when your expectations bear fruit you are right about how life is. If you believe "life is hard," you won't be surprised when things don't go your way. You can relax and feel safe about what to expect.

> It may be strange to think that you would rather have something bad happen simply because you expect it, than to have something good happen that would challenge your beliefs about how life is.

A lot of your beliefs are getting in the way of your happiness. This doesn't mean that there is something wrong with you. There is nothing wrong with you. Humans have beliefs and expectations about life. The question is not *whether* you have beliefs, but *what beliefs you have.* Yet there will be a part of you that will probably resist changing what you believe because it means changing how you see things, and then altering your response. Because you're human, change is not easy, but it is worth going through the hard part in order to allow yourself to have what you want. If you are willing to go through some discomfort to have what you want, you have the power to change your life.

> The question is not *whether* you have beliefs, but *what beliefs you have.*

*Your mother never told you...*
  *that changing the beliefs that aren't working for you will allow you to have the relationship you want.*

## How to Transform a Belief

You are already working toward shifting beliefs simply by becoming aware that you have them. In fact, awareness is ninety percent of the solution. Your relationships with men are bound to change if you follow our four simple steps to shifting a belief.

*Step one: Recognize that a thought you* think *is the truth is actually just a belief you are holding.*

At a cocktail party, Isabel found herself talking with James, an attractive and witty man whom she knew slightly through a mutual friend. She was really enjoying herself until an outgoing, good-looking woman drifted over and joined the conversation. After a few minutes Isabel found herself on the other side of the room. "Why did I leave?" she asked herself. "I'm interested in James, and he can't return my interest if I'm standing way over here."

"You won't be chosen," came the reply. Isabel looked over her shoulder, but it was her own mind that had provided the answer. She was shocked to discover that she was still having the same thought she'd had when she decided not to go out for the softball team in junior high, when she was waiting for a boy to ask her to prom in high school, and when she resisted her instructor's pleas to audition for a play in college. And this thought seemed like the truth to Isabel. Yet standing by the buffet table, it came to her that perhaps this thought was not the *truth*. Were there times when she *had* been chosen? In fact, once she started reviewing her life in her mind, she realized that she had indeed been chosen for many things: the national honor society, a good college, and a sorority. She had probably been more chosen than not chosen in her life. Yet she was living with the belief that she would not be chosen. Why would this be?

*Step two: Find the source of your belief. If you can't remember a specific incident, create a hypothesis by asking, "What might have happened to a little girl to have her believe that?"*

When Isabel got home after the party, she sat on the couch and looked at some photo albums to stimulate memories about her childhood. And as she flipped through the albums, some of the memories connected with this belief began surfacing. She remembered how traumatized she'd felt at age four when her brother was born, and how everyone's attention had shifted from her and onto him. She recalled that one afternoon she had started pulling books out of the bookcase when suddenly the shelf broke. The books thudded to the floor.

Frightened and hurt, Isabel had started to cry. "Mommy! Mommy!" she wailed.

"I'm feeding your brother," her mother called in an annoyed voice. "Come in here if you want to talk to me."

Isabel sat alone in the living room feeling dejected and thinking, "Mommy always chooses the baby over me." Looking back, Isabel remembered the fear, pain, and abandonment she'd experienced in that moment. Her mother had chosen to attend to her brother's needs before hers. Isabel felt certain that it was out of that incident that she had created the belief that she would never be chosen.

*Step three:* Notice how the belief influenced your decisions and choices.

Expecting she wouldn't be chosen gave Isabel a way to manage the overwhelming feeling of fear, pain, and abandonment her mother's response provoked. It also had her feel safe about the future, because knowing she wouldn't be chosen would enable her to survive a similar situation. In her girlhood, Isabel often retreated when a competition arose. She refused to compete because she wanted to spare herself the feeling of rejection that would remind her of the original experience. Later, as a young adult she continued her pattern of noncompetitiveness with men. If another woman became interested in a man Isabel was dating or even talking to, Isabel would simply walk away. In that way she lived out her belief that she wouldn't be chosen, because how could she be chosen if she was already out the door?

Recognizing how she had lived out her belief made Isabel sad, yet it also brought a lot of relief. If she'd missed being chosen by deciding she wasn't choosable, she could also be the one to change what kept happening to her. She could alter her belief. The next time she was talking to a man at a party and another woman came along, she could choose not to listen to her old belief. She could stay and talk to the man and see what happened.

*Step four: Remember that your belief is not the truth while changing the choices you make.*

A few weeks after the cocktail party, Isabel was invited to another party where she was pretty sure she would run into James again. She decided this was the perfect opportunity to try something different. Before the party she practiced saying in the mirror, "I am choosable, I will be chosen, men choose me." She felt nervous, but she was determined that if James showed up at the party, she would talk to him and not walk away—no matter how she felt or what went through her mind.

Sure enough, the moment Isabel walked into the party she spotted James. She took a deep breath and walked over to him. They immediately fell into the easy banter they'd enjoyed at the last party, and after a few minutes a woman in a pink dress sauntered over and joined in. Isabel felt a strong urge to move away, but she forced her feet to stay planted and her mouth to continue talking. Though it took every ounce of her energy to stay put, she managed to do it, ignoring the voice that was telling her to leave because she'd never be chosen over the woman in pink.

And then something miraculous happened: the other woman walked away, leaving Isabel alone with James. Stunned, Isabel realized she had stood her ground and acted like a woman who expected to be chosen. For the first time, she had acted consciously instead of letting her unconscious belief dictate her actions. And once she recognized that she'd broken through her belief, she wasn't surprised when James asked her to have dinner with him the next night.

Like Isabel, you have the power to change what happens by identifying and altering your beliefs. Being willing to be wrong about what you've decided about life or the beliefs you've formed, being willing to feel some discomfort as things start to change, and being willing to feel some sadness about the past will make the difference. You can take back the power to attract what you want into your life.

*You have the power to change what happens by identifying and altering your beliefs.*

*Your mother never told you...*
*that you have the power to change what you believe.*

*Think about...*

 **Notice how others live out their beliefs. Catch yourself in the act of living out a belief.**

*The exercises for Chapter Three can be found on page 263.*

# CHAPTER FOUR

# *Promises You Made*

### "But I Don't Want to Get Married ..."

In the mid-1980s when we were first developing a workshop on relationships, we decided to call it "So You Want to Get Married?" Because most single women around us said they wanted husbands, this seemed like a reasonable and even a catchy title. Eager to try it out, we approached ten single women who had often talked about marriage and said, "We're starting a workshop for women called, 'So You Want to Get Married?' Do you want to take the course?"

To our surprise, five of the ten women immediately blurted out, "But I *don't* want to get married!" They were just as startled as we were, and all of them followed up with a bewildered, "I've never said that before. Where did that come from?"

The responses of these five women provided a vivid example of how powerfully we can hide our motivations from ourselves. Each woman uncovered voices inside her that emphatically did not want what the woman thought she wanted to have. And until the voices that were resisting marriage unexpectedly spoke up, the women themselves had no idea that the voices existed—or that these dissenting voices might be a reason why they hadn't gotten married yet.

Francie, one of the five women, recalls that revealing her inner conflict changed her life.

"The funny thing is, I *absolutely* wanted to get married," she muses. "In fact, it had been a major focus of my work on myself for several years previously. Yet when my silent committee member finally spoke up, I discovered that wanting to get married wasn't my *only* truth. The larger truth was that I was conflicted and didn't realize it. So up until then I just couldn't understand why I hadn't found the relationship I wanted. Once I realized I had dissenting voices, I was able to listen to what they had to say, deal with their concerns, and free myself of their fears. A year later I met Liam, and we've been happily married for fourteen years now."

Uncovering a hidden conversation is like lifting a rock to see what's under it. You may be very surprised at what you find—and the results can be wonderful. When Francie found the dissenting committee members inside her and allowed them to have their say, she opened the way for Liam to come into her life. Like Francie, we are *all* motivated to some extent by hidden conversations—and once we identify them and address their concerns, our lives can open in ways we might not have imagined.

If you don't have what you want with a man, it may be because there is a part of you that *doesn't want it.* The voices that comprise your inner committee may seem unanimously in favor of having a relationship—but if you don't have one, there is a good chance that you have a silent committee member who is holding you back. Your silent committee member may have a resistance to relationship because she is trying to take care of you, and her motivations are healthy. A healthy human being stays away from a certain degree of pain and disappointment. Yet that committee member is also causing mischief by keeping quiet.

> We are *all* motivated to some extent by hidden conversations —and once we identify them and address their concerns, our lives can open in ways we might not have imagined.

Your silent committee members are the parts of you that have not recovered from past experiences of heartbreak. When a committee member doesn't speak up it is because she has taken a vow that she won't allow the painful experience to happen again. She's the one who keeps you from attending singles events or dating through the Internet. She's the one who is very picky and who tells you there are no good men left so you might as well not bother. She's the one who lets you assume there's something wrong with you when there is nothing wrong with you. She doesn't want you to get hurt again the way you were hurt before, and that is perfectly normal. Yet her resistance is holding you back—and if you don't uncover her voice, you may never be able to get past it.

> *Your mother never told you...*
> *that listening to your silent committee members*
> *could clear the path to having the relationship*
> *you want.*

## The Governor of Kentucky

On the second day of the "Having What You Want With a Man" Workshop, a group of women joined Debra, a Guidess, for lunch at a nearby deli. Trisha was pleased to be included in the group, because she had flown in from Kentucky and didn't know anyone. Feeling both tired and energized, she put her tray on the table next to Debra's and sat down with a sigh.

"I really should be eating salad," Trisha said ruefully as she crunched a potato chip. "My doctor said I should lose weight for the sake of my health. I really want to be thinner, but I just can't seem to get started on a diet and exercise program."

"That's interesting," Debra said, looking at her own plate of tuna salad. "What do you think is holding you back?"

"I'm not sure," Trisha said. "I wake up every morning determined to eat well and walk two miles, but by mid-afternoon I've lost all my motivation."

"Hmm," said Debra. "It sounds like you might be having a hidden conversation that's blocking you from making the choice to lose weight. Because it *is* a choice, right?"

"I guess so," said Trisha. "It seems like it just happens, but I must be making a choice at some point during the day."

"Sometimes making a different choice can be as simple as separating things your thoughts have linked," said Debra. "If you can uncover the hidden conversation you're having, you can separate the thoughts you've linked, and that will free you up to make a different choice."

> If you can uncover the hidden conversation you're having, you can separate the thoughts you've linked, and that will free you up to make a different choice.

Trisha frowned in concentration. "I'm not sure I quite understand what you're getting at," she said.

"Well, let's go through the process right now," said Debra. "First, tell me what you imagine life would be like if you were thin."

"Well, it goes like this," Trisha said, putting down her fork. "If I were thin I'd feel good about myself, and if I felt good about myself, I'd have the confidence to get involved with what interests me."

"It makes sense so far," said Debra. "Please go on."

"I want to help make the world a better place," said Trisha decisively.

"So then what?" Debra asked.

"So I'd start by getting involved in local politics."

"Then what?"

"If I got involved in local politics, I'd run for the school board."

"And then what?" Debra asked again.

"Then I would get involved in city planning and possibly the parks and recreation department, because I'm really interested in preserving the natural beauty of the land and educating the next generation about the importance of conservation."

"And then?"

"Then, if I got involved at the city level, I wouldn't be able to stop there. I'd have to then get involved in county politics."

"And then?"

"Then I'd run for a state senate seat. Eventually I'd be elected governor."

"Ah," said Debra. "So if you were thin, you'd be Governor of Kentucky."

Trisha grinned. "I've never quite made the connection myself before now, but I guess it's like this: I know if I got involved it would have to be in a big way. I think I'm really capable of being the governor. But I'm not ready to be the governor, and it's a really frightening prospect. So if I don't lose weight, I don't have to be the governor, because I won't feel good enough about myself to even work on a campaign."

"So because you have being thin linked in your mind with being the governor, you can't lose weight until you're ready to be out in the world in a big way," Debra mused.

"Yes, you're right."

"Revealing your hidden conversation lets you see that you have more than one choice: You could be heavy and still be the governor, you could be heavy and not be the governor, you could be thin and not be the governor, or you could be thin and be the governor," said Debra.

> Revealing your hidden conversation lets you see that you have more than one choice.

"Mm-hmm," agreed Trisha. "So I've been keeping myself overweight because of this unconscious link between my thoughts about being thin and my thoughts about being the governor."

"And now that you realize it, you can make a choice based on what's good for you rather than a choice based on a hidden conversation that's holding you back from having what you want," said Debra.

"So I could lose weight and *then* decide whether or not to run for office," said Trisha. "Well, *that's* a relief!"

"Wow," said Danielle, who was sitting across from Trisha, her sandwich forgotten in her hand as she listened. "This is really interesting. I think I have some of those unconscious links too."

"Everyone does," said Debra. "We all have hidden conversations that link two otherwise unrelated ideas and that keep us from making choices that are good for us."

"I wonder what mine are," Danielle mused.

"They can't be any more bizarre than mine," said Trisha, shaking her head.

"Well, why do you think you're not in a good relationship right now?" Debra asked Danielle.

"Umm ... I guess I'm just too busy for a relationship. I barely have a moment to myself as it is. I work full-time, help my sister take care of her two kids, volunteer at a nursing home, and moonlight as a musician."

"Goodness," said Trisha.

"So the reason you give yourself for not having a good relationship is that you're too busy," said Debra.

Danielle smiled. "I can tell you think that's not the real reason."

"Well, you are *choosing* not to be in a relationship," said Debra. "Being busy is often a secondary reason. What's the hidden conversation that's keeping you too busy to have a relationship?"

Danielle took a bite of her sandwich and chewed slowly. "I'm afraid that if I have a good relationship I'll turn into my mother."

"Good," said Debra. "That's a big one for a lot of women, actually. That, and 'If I have a good relationship with a man I'll lose my independence.'"

"And end up barefoot and pregnant," Trisha muttered.

"And have to give up my own interests," Danielle added.

"So the value of identifying these hidden conversations is that it helps you see you are making a choice," said Debra. "It may seem like the reason you're not in a relationship is that no good men are showing up—but the more subtle reason is that you're making a choice not to be in a relationship. Unconsciously you're choosing to stay single because you're afraid of turning into your mother, losing your independence, not being able to pursue your own interests, et cetera."

"It's a lot more powerful to see that we're making a choice, isn't it?" Danielle said. "If it's not just happening to us because we believe there aren't any good men out there. Because we are choosing it, then we can choose something else too."

"Exactly," said Debra. "You have the power of choice. And now I think we'd better choose to get going so we can go back and finish the Workshop!"

*Your mother never told you. . .*
*that uncovering your hidden conversations gives*
*you the power to make different choices.*

### Your "If ... Then" Conversations

Like Trisha and Danielle, you too have unconscious links between ideas that may be keeping you from having a relationship. An unconscious link is an "If ... then" conversation you are having with yourself, like the following examples.

*"If I get married, then I'll have to have children."*
*"If I love a man, then I'll have to do things his way."*
*"If I had a satisfying relationship, then I'd always have to be happy."*
*"If I found the man of my dreams, then I'd have to stop complaining."*
*"If I get married, then I'll never have time for my career."*
*"If I go out on a second date with him, then I'll have to marry him."*

 There Is No Prince

*"If I let him buy me dinner, then I'll have to be intimate with him."*

*"If I had plenty of love, then I'd have to start taking care of myself."*

*"If I got what I wanted, then it would be taken away."*

*"If I found a man to love me, then I'd lose my friends."*

*"If I'm successful financially, then I'll never find a man."*

*"If I marry him, then we'll have to be with his family instead of mine on holidays."*

*"If we get married, then I'd have ask him before I spend money."*

When you want something and you are worried about not getting it, it's good to check for any links your mind is making so you can free yourself to deal with the *real* issues that are standing in your way. Maybe you will discover a fear that loving a man means you will have to do things his way, for instance. It's powerful to recognize this fear so you can make a choice that will allow you to have the love you want while maintaining your autonomy. You can be awake from the beginning and catch yourself if you start giving in to a greater degree than is comfortable for you. You can then discuss what you want with your man, instead of worrying that you won't get it.

**When you reveal and heal your hidden motivations, they begin to lose their power.**

*Y̶our mother never told you. . .*
  *that you have the power to choose what is in your life.*

## Turning Up the Volume on Your Hidden Conversations

When you reveal and heal your hidden motivations, they begin to lose their power. If you are thinking, "I want it, I want it, I want it," and you don't have it—then you can assume there is an unheard conversation saying, "I don't want it for *this* reason. I don't want it because *that* terrible thing will happen. I don't want it because I vowed *never* to let it happen again." Tuning in to the conversations you haven't been hearing is a powerful way to clear away what is holding you back from having what you want with a man.

Francie wanted to get married more than anything in the world, but when she uncovered her hidden conversations she realized how conflicted she really was. "When I met Liam, I had constant committee meetings going on inside myself," she explains. "Most of my committee members were jumping up and down saying, 'Yes—he's the one. Go for it!' But I had some committee members who weren't crazy about the idea of commitment.

"'Remember what happened the last time,' said my cautious committee member. She was remembering the man I dated before Liam, who left on a trip to India, joined an ashram, and wrote me a letter saying he'd given up relationships.

"'Don't let yourself get hurt again,' said my scared committee member, referring to the man I thought would marry me when I was twenty-five—and who ended up marrying my best friend.

"'It's too much trouble to have a relationship, so why don't you just give up now?' asked my resigned committee member—the one who thought it could never happen for me.

"At first I was afraid to hear the conflicting opinions of my dissenting committee members. It seemed like if I gave them too much credit, their views of my relationship would come true. Working with Marilyn helped me get over that fear. She reassured me that it might be uncomfortable for a while, but that listening to my committee members would actually free me up to have the relationship I wanted with Liam.

**When voices conflict it doesn't necessarily mean one is true and the other is not.**

"After a while I found the courage to listen to all my committee members. I imagined that I was talking with each one of them and explained gently that I knew Liam was different from other men in my past.

I explained that I had grown since my last relationship, and that it could really work this time. And it was amazing how my heart opened. I felt like there was suddenly all this extra room inside—room for me to move ahead with my relationship."

## Honoring All the Voices

Francie discovered that when voices conflict it doesn't necessarily mean one is true and the other is not. It means *they are all true and they are not aligned* with each other. So you can want to get married *and* not want to get married. You can desire to be intimate *and* be afraid of intimacy. You can want closeness *and* need a lot of distance. One voice does not invalidate the other.

Putting your hidden conversations on loudspeaker allows them to be integrated into your awareness. When you tune in to all your conversations, you can work with *all* the aspects of yourself rather than only *some* of them. Your committee members all have valid concerns and deserve to have their say. You may be having conversations like: "I want it." "I don't want it." "I'm afraid of losing my freedom." "I'm afraid of being vulnerable." "I'm afraid of being left." and "It reminds me of the past." Revealing these conversations frees you to deal with the real issues at hand. And when you reveal the conversations, old issues may disappear, such as choosing a man who is not good for you, deciding that all men are commitment-phobic. And you will no longer think there is something wrong with you because you don't have what you want.

Turning up the loudspeaker to hear your real conflicts means you will probably have to feel the feelings associated with them. If you discover that you are afraid of being close to someone because your mother smothered you with closeness when you were a child, you may begin to feel fear brought on by someone's proximity. If you find you are angry with men because your father treated you badly, you may begin to feel anger at being mistreated.

"Revealing my hidden conversations allowed me to deal with

the feelings I'd kept buried," says Francie. "Until I uncovered them, I had been feeling only the feelings that resulted from *hiding* the conversation—rather than the original fear or pain that the conversations were based on. I was constantly frustrated at not finding a good man. I was lonely and criticized myself for not having what I wanted.

"Keeping the hidden conversations buried didn't actually keep me from feeling bad—it just kept me from dealing with the real issues. I was searching for outward solutions rather than focusing on what was really holding me back. And once I opened the conversation and felt the feelings associated with them, I could let the feelings move through me and disappear."

**Accepting your internal conflict allows you to come up with a creative solution.**

Accepting your internal conflict allows you to come up with a creative solution. You can attend to the concerns of all your committee members by asking new questions that include both the desire and the committee member's worry—questions such as:

> *"How can I be in a relationship while still having enough time for myself?"*
> *"How can I maintain my own financial security while joining lives with someone else?"*
> *"How can I feel better about myself while I go through the trial and error of dating?"*
> *"How can I be open to loving someone else while making sure I take care of myself?"*

This new kind of questioning will help you have what you want. A world of possibilities for how to be in relationship will open up for you, and you will be able to experience more optimism. The beliefs that have been holding you back may naturally melt away as you take an active part in finding a creative solution.

Having a healthy conversation with yourself gives you the opportunity to design the relationship you want.

*Your mother never told you...*
  *that your conflicting voices are valid expressions of different parts of you.*

## Encountering Resistance

Thirty-six-year-old Tanya had a pattern of dating men in their mid-50s, until she entered a relationship with Brad, a man her own age. For two months things were going well, then Tanya started to notice that something didn't feel right. She signed up for a guiding session.

"I've been feeling really strange about the man I'm seeing," Tanya said.

"What's up?"

"Well, I don't really know. I've just been feeling ... uncomfortable."

"What do you mean by uncomfortable? Is everything going OK?" Sara looked concerned.

"Oh, it's great. Couldn't be better, in fact. He fits all the lists I made at the Workshop—you know, what's crucial that a man must have and not have in order for me to get seriously involved with him. If my mother were still alive I know she'd really like him."

"So what is it that's uncomfortable for you?" Sara asked gently.

"Well, I'm excited about the way things are going, but I also dread going out with him. And when I think about the future, I get nauseous. Usually I can create a detailed picture of the future, but when I think about the future with Brad, I just draw a blank. I can't visualize us having a life together, and that bothers me because I really like him."

Tanya bit her lip and looked down at her hands. She laced her fingers together and watched them fold and unfold.

"Tanya," said Sara gently. "Something else is going on here. If you can share with me what it is, we may be able to get to the bottom of your discomfort."

Tanya took a deep breath and looked up at the poster on the far wall. It was a painting of a heart in many layers of pink and purple. She felt the pain in her own heart and knew she had to face what was difficult in order to heal. Suddenly it became clear to her what had been haunting her.

"I got pregnant when I was sixteen," she said softly. "I was living in a small town in Michigan. It just wasn't okay to walk around my school with a huge belly, even in the eighties. It was awful. My parents made me give up the baby for adoption."

"That must have been really hard for you," said Sara softly. "Such a big thing to happen for a young girl, and you didn't have any support."

Tanya blotted her eyes with a tissue. "I don't know how I lived through it. You're the first person I've talked to about this. I guess I sealed it off—from myself as well as from others. It's such a relief to talk about it."

"I'm sure it is," Sara said. "And now that it's out in the open, we can find out how your early experience is affecting what's in your life today."

"Good," Tanya said. "I know it's been holding me back."

Sara nodded. "It sounds like the scared sixteen-year-old that you were is still inside you, feeling the same pain she felt back then. You'll remember from the Workshop that we all have many aspects of ourselves, and some of those aspects are younger versions of ourselves that have been frozen in time. Each aspect of ourselves has a voice, and they are often in conversation with each other."

"Yes," said Tanya.

"The sixteen-year-old you didn't have the resources to deal with the pain she was feeling, so it is likely that she was frozen by the trauma of getting pregnant and giving up her baby. Because she couldn't deal with her situation then, she retreated into herself. And she's holding you back because she's afraid of being hurt again."

"That sounds pretty likely," said Tanya, sniffling.

"That traumatized sixteen-year-old has a voice—a voice that you haven't been able to hear for many years because as you said, you'd sealed that part of you off. If you turn up the volume now, you may be able to hear what she's saying. Once you can hear her, you can help her heal her pain. And when she is healed, she won't be holding you back from having what you want with a man anymore. So just let yourself lean back, breathe, and listen to that traumatized part of yourself."

Tanya closed her eyes and put her hand over her heart, listening within. She breathed deeply and felt her attention turning inward to a tender place in her heart that had been hurting for a long time.

"She's saying I don't deserve to have children," Tanya whispered. "She wants me to stay away from the subject of having a family and not let anyone get close enough to bring it up. She's taken a vow never to get pregnant again and she's afraid that if I get involved with someone I'll break it."

"Mmm," Sara murmured. "That would have been something wise for the sixteen-year-old to decide. She was doing her best to protect herself from being hurt in the future."

Tanya kept her eyes closed, listening to Sara's quiet voice.

"You've just discovered what we call a *hidden conversation*," Sara continued. "It's great that you could tune into it. A hidden conversation is when one or more of the voices inside you isn't speaking up loudly enough for you to hear it. And because that voice stays silent, it motivates you powerfully without you realizing it."

"I've been avoiding the question of having children for a long time, haven't I?" Tanya asked.

"It sure looks that way," said Sara. "Dating men in their 50s might have been a way to keep you from having to face your dilemma," Sara smiled. "Why don't you think about it this week and try to come up with the hidden conversation your silent committee member has been having. Write in your journal and we'll talk about what you discover next week. Be sure to think about that precious sixteen-year-old and hold her softly in your heart."

Tanya spent a lot of time by herself the next week, meditating and getting in touch with her inner committee. "Be careful, you've been hurt before," warned one voice. "It's too much effort, why don't you just forget it?" said another. Tanya listened to their concerns and wrote them in her journal. Once they were written down they didn't seem so serious. In fact, they seemed almost trivial compared to the positive aspects of her deepening relationship with Brad.

## Revealing Your Hidden Conversation

By her next meeting with Sara, Tanya was pretty sure she'd identified the hidden conversation she'd been having for so many years. She sat in her usual chair and pulled out her journal.

"Here goes," she said. "I guess my hidden conversation went something like this: 'If I date men in their thirties, they will want me to have children and I don't know if I want that. It's too painful for me to have to face that question, and I can avoid it by dating men who are over fifty and probably won't want kids with me.' In fact, a lot of men I dated were divorced and already had children of their own. How clever of me! It was a great way to stay far away from the pain and shame I experienced before."

**Simply revealing a hidden conversation is enough to diminish its power over you.**

"Simply revealing a hidden conversation is enough to diminish its power over you," said Sara. "Sometimes noticing it is all you need to do. Yet to fully heal, it helps to have a conversation with your silent committee member—in this case, the traumatized teenager inside you. You can soothe her and reassure her that things are different now. You can share with her the wisdom you've gained in the past twenty years. And you can open your heart to her. Ask her what she needs from you in order for her to feel safe. I suggest you take some time at home tonight to talk with her. Get really comfortable in bed or on the sofa, and have a conversation with her."

"Okay, I will," said Tanya. "Thanks, Sara."

When she got home, Tanya changed into her favorite cotton pajamas. She brewed herself a cup of hot cocoa and settled herself in bed, propped up against several pillows. She turned off her reading lamp and lit a few candles so the room was suffused with a warm glow. Then she leaned back and put her hand on her heart, closing her eyes and breathing deeply. Soon she felt the pain surface as it had when she looked at the heart poster in Sara's office.

"I understand your pain," she said. "Your pain is real and you have every right to feel it. But things are different now."

Tanya pictured her sixteen-year-old self sitting next to her on the bed. She imagined putting her arm around her.

"What would you need in order to feel safe?" Tanya asked.

"I need to know it will all be different next time," her sixteen-year-old self responded. Tanya felt her heart swelling with compassion.

"We're thirty-six now—we're a grown woman," she explained gently. "If we got pregnant now it would be totally different than it was back then. What can I reassure you about?"

"Tell me what it would be like," said her sixteen-year-old self.

"We would have a man to love us and help us through it, a man who would commit to taking care of the child with us. He would be a good father and his parents wouldn't force him to abandon us the way Sam's parents did. And *our* dad wouldn't be angry at us this time. In fact, he would be thrilled to have a grandchild. We could keep the baby and bring her up in a stable, loving environment with a mother, a father, grandparents, and lots of other people to dote on her."

"Really?" asked her sixteen-year-old self.

"I promise," Tanya said.

Tanya felt her heart swelling and opening. Suddenly she was sobbing into her pillow, letting out all the grief she'd kept inside for so many years. After a few minutes her pillow was wet and the pain had subsided.

"I can have a mature relationship with a man my own age," Tanya said out loud. "And I can decide when and if I want to have children." She blew her nose, wiped her eyes, and took a sip of the comforting cocoa.

Tanya breathed a sigh of relief. She felt peaceful inside, as if a tension she'd been carrying around with her had been lifted. She went to the bathroom and splashed cold water on her face, then looked in the mirror.

"We're going to be all right," she said to her reflection. And for the first time, she knew it was true.

*Your mother never told you...*
*that you are motivated by inner conversations*
*you didn't even know you were having.*

## The Vows We Take

When Tanya turned up the volume on her hidden conversation, she was astounded to discover how powerfully the vow she took at sixteen was still affecting what she allowed into her life at age thirty-six. Once *you* start looking for hidden conversations, you too may be amazed to discover the extent to which your life can be run by vows you took in the past.

Vows you took may have included any of the following:

*"I'll never be like my mother."*
*"I'll never be trapped in a marriage."*

*"I want to find a man just like my father."*

*"I'll never marry a man like my father."*

*"I'll never go through a divorce."*

*"I'll never have children."*

*"I'll never be vulnerable."*

*"I'll never let a man get in the way of my career."*

*"I'll never get hurt like that again."*

*"I'll never hurt a man like that again."*

The vows we take make sense because we are trying to protect ourselves from being hurt like we were before. Yet they actually hurt us *more* by becoming beliefs that hold us back from having what we want. Some vows are based on hidden conversations that are fairly universal to women today because they are based on our collective history—and some are based on our individual history.

It is likely that you have a committee member who equates being loved with losing her freedom. This is a fairly universal hidden conversation for women that makes a lot of sense based on our collective past. It wasn't long ago that it was expected a woman would give up most of her freedom when she got "hitched" to a man. Until recently, we automatically changed our names, moved wherever his job took us, and of course stayed home with our children. It's no wonder we might be having hidden conversations warning us not to give up our freedom.

Tanya's vow never to get pregnant again stopped her from having a good relationship with someone her own age.

Once *you* start looking for hidden conversations, you too may be amazed to discover the extent to which your life can be run by vows you took in the past.

To keep her vow, she unconsciously chose older men. Once she discovered the vow she took, she could dissolve her belief and create a new belief that allowed her to have power—and choice—back in her own life.

Like Tanya, if you are not aware of what is holding you back you may find yourself coming up with a reason you don't have what you want that may have *nothing to do with the real reason.* You may end up feeling like a helpless victim in your own life—rather than a powerful woman who can attract the man and the relationship she wants.

You've probably forgotten some of the vows you took. If you want to uncover what they are, take a look at what you have in your life right now. If you don't have what you want with a man, you probably took a vow that's keeping you from having it. Exploring your history and discovering your beliefs will help you find the hidden conversations that are holding you back. Hidden conversations don't just disappear. The committee member who took the vow holds onto it until, as Tanya did, you can have a loving conversation with her and help her heal the original experience.

*Your mother never told you...*
*that you can help yourself have what you want*
*by uncovering your hidden conversations and*
*healing the original pain.*

### "But What Would My Parents Think?"

How would your parents feel if you had an extraordinary relationship? Some of our most limiting hidden conversations are based on reactions to our parents and their responses to our success and happiness. We all want to think that our parents would be happy for us if we got what we want and indeed, on one level, they probably would be. Yet on another level they might be threatened by our happiness.

"When I started having a good relationship with Liam, it was hard on my relationship with my mother," recalls Francie. "I was having the kind of relationship that she had probably always dreamed of having—an equal, loving, nurturing partnership. I could tell that she wanted to support me, but it was eating her up inside. She kept making little snide comments about Liam and implying that I was too old to get married. But I could see that she was watching us interact and paying attention to how I was dealing with issues that came up.

"Eventually my mother started asking me questions about my relationship, and I realized she was learning about how to have a good relationship from me. And that felt strange to both of us, because it was the reverse of how we thought it was supposed to be. *I* should have learned about good relationships from *her*. But my parents had a very distant, formal relationship without a lot of loving communication. So my closeness with Liam was a break in our family style. In the end, it benefited both of us because I could see that she made some small changes in how she related to my father."

When you have what you want, it forces your parents to examine their own relationship, and this could be uncomfortable for them—as it was for Francie's mother. And because you are a good girl you don't want your parents to be uncomfortable. You don't want them to experience regret about their lives, to feel badly about themselves, or to feel jealous of you. So keeping your parents safe becomes a hidden conversation that goes something like, "If I don't have a better relationship than *they* had, they won't have to feel bad. Everything remains status quo and I continue to be a good daughter." The problem is that the conversation keeps you from having the great relationship you want and deserve.

Some of us are also keeping ourselves unhappy deliberately in order to punish our parents. Even if you don't realize it, there's a good chance that you are angry with your parents on some level. Well-intentioned as they may be, at some point in your childhood they embarrassed you, humiliated you, didn't give you what you wanted, or weren't the way you needed them to be.

As Tanya continued to work with Sara, she discovered she was still angry with her parents for forcing her to give up her baby for adoption. Her vow never to get pregnant again was partly made as a punishment for her parents. Her sixteen-year-old committee member was having the conversation, "I don't want my father to experience the joy of having grandchildren because he deprived me of my first baby." Uncovering that hidden conversation allowed Tanya to forgive her parents for their decision and give herself permission to get close to someone who was interested in having children.

> Understanding *why* you have what you have allows you to be more optimistic about the future and know things can be different from how they have always been.

Like Tanya, you may well have a silent committee member who wants to get back at your parents by not being happy and successful in the way they would like you to be. Until you can unearth the silent committee member and listen to her vow, you might keep yourself unhappy in order to get back at your parents. It's worth doing a little digging to see if you unearth hidden conversations like, "I want to keep my parents feeling safe," or "I don't want my parents to feel good." There's a good chance you are motivated unconsciously by one or both of these conversations.

Denying yourself is a way to keep the family dynamic intact. To find out the extent to which you are sacrificing your own happiness to keep things comfortable in your family, ask yourself the following questions:

*"How happy can I be and still be a member of my family?"*
*"How good a marriage can I have and still be a member of my family?"*
*"How cherished can I be by a man and still be a member of my family?"*
*"How balanced between work and family can I have my life be, and still be a member of my family?"*

If the answer is *"Not very,"* you can create a new, positive conversation for yourself that supports your happiness. Understanding *why* you have what you have allows you to be more optimistic about the future and know things can be different from how they have always been. You can find compassion for the parts of you that have been hurt, and being tender with yourself opens your heart. When your heart is open, you won't be holding things against yourself, and you will be more available to receive love. Then, both loving a man and being loved by him will be easier.

*Your mother never told you. . .*
 *that you would have hidden conversations based on not wanting to change the family dynamic.*

*Think about. . .*

 **What vows you might have made.**

*The exercises for Chapter Four can be found on page 264.*

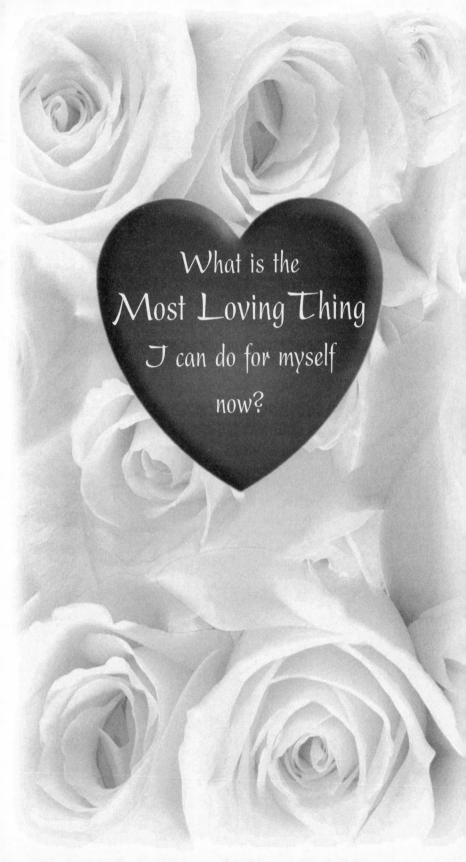

What is the **Most Loving Thing** I can do for myself now?

# CHAPTER FIVE

# *Finding a Man Begins With...*

Loving yourself—treating yourself with generosity, nurturing your needs and desires, and forgiving yourself for human mistakes—is the most important concept we teach at Life Works. It is also the most important tool you have for enjoying the relationship you want, and one of the most subtle. We consider this chapter the cornerstone of all the work in this book. The message is simple, and when you can absorb it your life will change and become more satisfying—perhaps without you even noticing it.

In this chapter, we include the story of Gemma, who is really a composite of many women who have taken our "Having What You Want With a Man" workshop. Her story is longer than any of the others you will read in this book, but it contains several important examples of being self-loving—and what can come from it—that we hope will inspire you.

At the end of our "Having What You Want With a Man" workshops, we give every woman in the course a magnet. It reads:

*What is the most loving thing I can do for myself now?*

That magnet is for women to put on their refrigerators, their bathroom mirrors, or wherever they'll see it often. Because if you ask yourself that question every day, even many times a day if you can, it will remind you to keep your heart open and listen to yourself.

*What is the most loving thing I can do for myself now?* is not a question we were taught to ask. Most of us learn to ask ourselves things such as, "Am I doing it well enough?" "Have I done it fast enough?" and "How am I doing compared to my friends?" And most of all, we ask, "What's wrong with me?" But when you are asking yourself what is the most loving thing you can do for yourself, you can't possibly answer that something is wrong with you.

> When you are asking yourself what is the most loving thing you can do for yourself, you can't possibly answer that something is wrong with you.

We all tend to think that when things aren't going our way, there's something wrong with us. But when you are asking yourself a loving question, you can't come up with that answer. You can change your relationship with yourself by the questions you ask—and when your relationship with yourself shifts, your life will never be the same.

Many of our problems come from feeling a lack of love and looking outside ourselves to fill it. We do all sorts of crazy things when we're not loving ourselves enough. We try to find fulfillment through work, or making money, or having a man love us. We think that if only a man would come along and make it all better, we would be happy. And we think that almost any man will do. But it doesn't work—because we're not having a heartfelt relationship with ourselves. We need to love ourselves before looking for love from a man.

When you're busy holding grudges against yourself—for something you might have said, or not done, or a mistake you made, even if it was long ago—and when you're angry or disappointed in yourself, you don't allow yourself to have what you want. It really is that simple. Think of giving people gifts at holiday time. If you're not happy with someone, you probably don't want to give them a gift. And if they're pleasing you, you want to get them something really nice.

We treat ourselves the same way. To the extent that we're angry with ourselves and disappointed in ourselves, we don't give ourselves good things. If one of the good things you want is a relationship with a man, you won't allow yourself to have it if you're holding grudges against yourself.

Don't worry if you feel you can't absorb all of these concepts right away. You can start to change your life just by being nicer to yourself, and more forgiving. Loving yourself is a practice. It's a practice of asking yourself, "What's the most loving thing I can do for myself now?" It also means being patient. Above all, loving yourself means knowing there is nothing wrong with you.

*Your mother never told you. . .*
*the most important relationship you'll ever have*
*is with yourself.*

## Making Yourself Happy

Gemma glanced at the clock as she pulled on her pumps. Six forty-five. Good, she could catch the next train and be at her desk by seven-thirty. Maybe she'd even have time to grab a cup of coffee at the station. She was feeling a little tired. As she checked her hair in the bathroom mirror, her eyes fell on the heart-shaped magnet at the corner of the medicine cabinet. It had been there for two months since she'd taken the "Having What You Want With a Man" workshop. She'd been diligently asking herself every day, "What's the most loving thing I can do for myself now?"

Gemma had started to really look forward to asking herself that question. Sometimes she asked it in the morning as her day began, sometimes at work when she was in the middle of a stressful meeting, and other times when she got home at eight o'clock at night. Every time she asked it, she felt her heart open a little—and often an answer would come to her. She would call her best friend Bette for moral support before work, take a five-minute break from her meeting to sit in a bathroom stall and breathe, or take a bubble bath before bed.

Suddenly Gemma felt overcome by exhaustion. She braced herself with both hands on the edge of the sink and stared at her reflection in the mirror.

"Pale, pasty skin," she said to herself. "Dark circles under my eyes. Haunted look of an overworked city professional." She took a deep breath. "What's the most loving thing I can do for myself now?"

As she stared into her eyes, Gemma felt a smile starting at the corners of her mouth. "You know, I think I'm going to get back in bed," she said to her reflection. "I am absolutely, utterly exhausted. I've been working twelve to sixteen hours a day for ten years. I've hardly ever gotten into the office after eight a.m., never mind taking a day off."

Gemma kicked off her shoes, shook her hair out of its neat chignon, slipped out of her suit, and climbed back into her unmade bed. Pulling the comforter up under her chin, she stretched luxuriously. "I think I'm taking a personal day," she said. Then she sat straight up. "Goodness, who said that! Certainly not Gemma the workaholic success-driven career woman!" She snuggled back into the pillows, giggling.

When Gemma awoke again at ten-thirty, she felt wonderfully refreshed. After going down to the corner café for coffee and a croissant, she found herself wandering around her apartment. "Gosh, I never realized how half-lived-in this place looks," she thought. "I'm hardly ever here during the day. The living room could use a coat of paint, and there's a lot of clutter that I'd like to clean out. I would just love to have the time to create a nurturing space for myself." She allowed her mind to wander, imagining her apartment filled with plants, colorful cushions, and soft lighting.

There Is No Prince

"And I want to paint the kitchen yellow," Gemma thought. "A soft, buttery yellow. Beef up my kitchen supplies—and learn to cook! Imagine, me giving dinner parties. People coming over to share in the welcoming, feminine space I've created." She felt like jumping up and down. She knew she could do it—she could create the home she wanted.

"I guess I was waiting for a man to come into my life to do all that," Gemma mused to Peg, a Guidess at Life Works, at their next session. "I think inwardly I just believed that once I was married, I would suddenly become more domestic and take the time to create a warm environment for us. But taking that day off to be alone at my place was a revelation. Like you said, I need to allow myself to have good things. And I'm going to do it!"

Peg grinned. "That's great, Gemma," she said. "You've come a long way in the two months we've been seeing each other. You know what you are starting to do?"

"Take better care of myself?" ventured Gemma.

"Yes, definitely," said Peg. "You are beginning to build a loving, warmhearted relationship with yourself. It was a big step for you to take a day off from work. And to realize you can have what you want *now*, without waiting for a man to give it to you. Which he may not even be able to do, right?"

Gemma nodded. "I'm not really thinking about men right now," she said. "It feels so good to be doing loving things for myself. I bought myself a necklace I've been eyeing at Macy's for at least three months. And I just can't wait to start working on my apartment. I've already looked at paint samples and copper-bottomed pans to hang over the island in the kitchen. I'm going to make time in my schedule to sign up for a cooking class. I'm so excited!"

The next few months were very full for Gemma. She painted her living room a soft peach color and her kitchen butter yellow. She bought cushions in bright jewel tones for the loveseat, large leafy plants to filter the light, and hung her shiny new pans in the kitchen. She started a cooking class at the local culinary arts school twice a week, and even found the time to walk twenty minutes to and from the class for exercise. She slept an hour later in the mornings, and to her surprise found that getting to work at eight-thirty rather than seven-thirty was actually beneficial to her performance. Because she was better rested, she was more efficient and alert and got the same amount of work done in less time.

"I'm giving my first dinner party tonight," Gemma told Peg at one of their sessions. "I'm so excited. I'm making chicken cordon bleu, roasted rosemary potatoes, and asparagus." She shook her head. "Four months ago I never would have imagined I'd be doing this."

"You are doing just great," Peg said. "You are developing a loving, supportive relationship with yourself—getting more rest, some exercise, creating a nest for yourself, and now sharing it with your friends. It's really inspiring, Gemma."

"I feel like I'm really caring for myself for the first time ever," Gemma said.

"Yes," said Peg. "And taking care of yourself now means that once you get into a relationship you won't have to push men away by finding something wrong with them. You'll feel safer because you will be able to trust that you will take care of yourself. Getting to know and love yourself means you won't have to worry about losing yourself in a relationship like your mother did. You'll care too much for yourself to allow anything bad to happen to you—and if something begins to go wrong, you'll catch it in the nick of time."

"Yes, I think you're right," Gemma said. But she found it hard to think about a relationship at the moment. Her mind was on the dinner party. What sort of flowers should she buy for the table? Did she remember to ask Bette to bring some white wine? Oh, and Larry had asked if he could bring his friend Jules, who had just moved to town. She must remember to make enough food for seven people instead of six.

There Is No Prince

*Your mother never told you...*
*you could be in relationship without losing*
*yourself.*

## When You're Ready, He Will Come

A week later, Gemma sat on the edge of the big easy chair in Peg's office, scarcely able to contain her excitement.

"I take it the dinner party went well," Peg said, taking in Gemma's radiant face and tapping feet.

"Oh, it was a disaster," Gemma said. "The chicken got completely dried out and I used the wrong cheese so it was all gooey. I forgot about the potatoes and they burned to a crisp, and the asparagus was practically raw because I was so paranoid I'd overcook it. We tried to eat it but after everyone made a valiant attempt, we just started laughing. We dove into the wine and I ordered pizzas. It turned out to be the most fun I've had in ages. And ..." she paused dramatically. "I met a man!"

Peg grinned. "You go girl! He was at the party?"

"Yes," said Gemma. "My friend Larry brought a friend of his named Jules. Isn't that the most lovely name? He grew up in England but he's lived here since college. Anyway, Jules had just moved to town. He works at Larry's engineering firm. He's a mechanical engineer, he's thirty-six, wears these great wire-rimmed glasses, and works out regularly. He's really funny, too, with that dry kind of wit, very English. We hit it off right away, and he ended up asking me to go to the movies with him the next night. In fact, we've had three dates in the past week. Can you believe it?"

### Men show up when you're ready.

"Well, yes, actually," said Peg. "You've been doing such a wonderful job of developing your relationship with yourself that I had a hunch the right man would be coming into your life sometime soon. That's when it happens, you know—when you're taking good care of yourself, loving yourself, and involved in your own life. Men show up when you're ready. Do you realize how much you've changed in the last few months?"

Gemma sighed and closed her eyes. "Hmm. Well, yes, I guess I *have* changed. I feel like it's not so much a change as a ... I don't know exactly how to put it ... a coming into myself. Like becoming more of who I am, you know? Not putting myself into a box, allowing the softer parts of me to come out. And the more I do that, the more I fall in love with myself."

> When you're in love with yourself, you're irresistible.

"Exactly," said Peg. "And when you're in love with yourself, you're irresistible. As you just discovered."

We have often been trained, by our mothers or by the culture, that loving ourselves—thinking of our needs, asking for what we want—is selfish. But loving ourselves is the opposite of being selfish, as hard as that may be to believe at first. Selfish means not taking other people into consideration. It's a word that implies a lack of something, or an insecurity about something. Being "selfish" is a reaction to not being loved or being afraid of not getting enough love. Self-love is a heartfelt expression of compassion, tenderness, gentleness, forgiveness, generosity, and gratefulness. It means giving yourself the benefit of the doubt, knowing you are doing the best you can, allowing things to take the time they take, and being inspired by your own struggle. It means holding your own hand through the hard parts of life.

When you're self-centered, it means you're only thinking about yourself: How does this affect me? What am I going to get out of this? Et cetera. But when you are truly loving yourself, everyone benefits. You have an open heart and you can receive the love others want to give you—and you have a lot of love to share with them, too. And you can help someone else give you what *you* want. Then they feel great for giving you what you want, and you feel great because you have what you want. Loving yourself means having enough to be able to be generous to others.

## Keeping Your Heart Open

In the following months, Gemma started to see a lot of Jules. They went to museums, ate luxurious lunches at fancy restaurants, saw movies, and took long walks together. Jules was a good cook, as it turned out, and they often spent time in the kitchen. They laughed together constantly.

Gemma marveled to herself that it seemed so much easier than it ever had before. She found that she was enjoying herself in the moment and not always worrying about what had happened or what was going to happen. If Jules showed up ten minutes late, she didn't hold it against him. If she found herself saying something critical, she was able to catch herself and apologize immediately. It all seemed to flow much more naturally than she had ever imagined possible.

"A lot of it is because I'm still taking care of myself," she confided to her friend Bette one evening. "I'm taking time apart from Jules to be with my friends, like tonight. I also make sure to spend at least one evening a week alone at home, so I can enjoy the environment I've created for myself. I even cook myself good dinners. And I decided I needed some meditation and exercise, so when my cooking classes ended I signed up for a yoga class three mornings a week. It really helps me feel relaxed, centered, and strong. And it helps me keep my connection to myself."

## Stumbling on the Way to the Altar

A few months later, it was a perfect autumn Sunday in the city, the gold and red leaves dropping lazily from the trees and swirling down in the gentle cool breeze. Gemma and Jules were walking hand in hand through the park, swishing through piles of fallen leaves and watching children playing tag and flying kites. Gemma felt a swelling sense of well being, a pink balloon of happiness expanding in her heart. She rested her head briefly on Jules' strong shoulder, relishing the kiss he planted on her hair.

"What a perfect day, isn't it?" she asked.

"Absolutely brilliant," said Jules. "I don't think I've ever been this happy."

"Me neither," Gemma agreed.

Jules squeezed Gemma's hand and cleared his throat. "In fact, er, I've been thinking," he said. "We've been together for more than six months now. We're a perfect match, you and I. I've never had so much fun with anyone in my life. And I love you."

"I love you, too," said Gemma, looking into Jules' dark green eyes. Suddenly her feelings were too overwhelming. She felt the urge to run. "Try and catch me!" she called, sprinting across the grass and kicking up clouds of red and yellow leaves. Jules ran after her and pulled her down into a pile of leaves. They lay side by side, laughing breathlessly. Suddenly two small boys charged past them, yelling and throwing a football back and forth.

"Would you like a couple of those, Gem?" Jules asked, stroking her hair. "When we get married, we'll have a couple of real hellions, eh? And girls, too, tons of them."

Gemma sat up abruptly. "Yes, well, umm," she said. "Listen, I'm hungry. Didn't you promise me brunch?" She stood, brushing leaves and grass off of her jeans, and started walking in the direction of their favorite café across the park.

"Hey, wait up!" Jules caught her hand. "Why the sudden hurry? Was it something I said?"

"No, of course not," said Gemma. "I'm just hungry, that's all. Getting a sugar low, I guess."

They walked on quietly, but suddenly Gemma felt his hand pulling against hers. She wondered if he wanted something, but he was looking out across the pond to their left. His hand kept pulling regularly, every time he took a step. She looked at his legs and noticed that he lurched slightly as he walked. Perhaps his left leg was a little shorter than his right. He had a rather strange rolling gait, actually. Funny that she'd never noticed it before. She couldn't stop staring at the way he walked, and when he noticed her watching him she looked away quickly. She felt the expansive balloon of happiness in her heart begin to deflate. It felt like her heart was closing, shrinking in on itself. She felt like she could barely breathe.

"Is everything okay?" asked Jules, looking at her with concern.

"Um, I'm not feeling so great," said Gemma. "I think I'd better go home."

"Shall I get a taxi?" Jules asked.

"Oh no, I can walk. It's only a few blocks," said Gemma.

"Here, I'll give you a piggyback ride," said Jules playfully.

"No, really, Jules. I'll go by myself. You go and have brunch, I'll be fine." Gemma just had to get away from him. She took off at a brisk pace, waving at him as he stood underneath a red maple tree with a puzzled look on his face.

That night Gemma couldn't sleep. She tossed and turned, getting all twisted up in her new damask sheets. Finally she sat up and turned on the light.

"It's his walk," she said to herself. "How could I have overlooked it before? I was blinded by infatuation. He walks like … like a freak! He lurches like Quasimodo. No wonder things have been going well. He was thrilled to find someone who could overlook his walk at last. But how can I keep overlooking it now that I've noticed? I can't marry him. Imagine us walking down the aisle, everyone snickering behind their hands. Oh no, what am I going to do?"

Gemma could barely concentrate at work the next day. She found herself staring out the window, thinking about Jules and his walk. When it was finally five o'clock, she rushed to Life Works for her weekly appointment with Peg.

"I have to break up with him," Gemma blurted out.

Peg shook her head in confusion. "What? But it's been going so well, you've been taking care of yourself, he's been responding in kind, and you're in love. What happened?"

"Well, nothing really happened." Gemma leaned forward and said in a half-whisper, "It's his walk."

"His walk?"

"Yes. I can't believe I never noticed it before. Jules walks like Quasimodo—you know, the Hunchback of Notre Dame? He lurches, it's awful. Just awful. There's no way I can be with someone who lurches. I'm just going to have to think of some way to say it so I don't hurt his feelings."

Peg pressed her lips together, studying Gemma. "Okay, listen. I want you to sit back, close your eyes, and breathe deeply for a couple of minutes," she instructed in a no-nonsense voice.

Gemma obeyed. To her annoyance, she felt a throbbing in her heart as she began to breathe. It was as if her heart wanted to expand, but she fiercely refused to let it. She wouldn't give in, she wouldn't settle for someone who was so clearly flawed. She deserved better.

"Now tell me exactly what happened," said Peg.

"We were walking in the park yesterday, and it was beautiful. Everything was just perfect until I felt his hand sort of pulling on mine. I thought he wanted to get my attention, but he was looking away. Then I noticed that he had this uneven gait that made his hand jerk when he walked. It was repulsive. I started to feel awful, and I told him I was sick and had to go home."

"And what happened right before you noticed his walk?" Peg looked at Gemma over the top of her reading glasses.

"Before? I don't know, nothing really," said Gemma. "Oh yes, we told each other we loved each other."

"But that's nothing new, you've been saying that for a few months now, right?" asked Peg.

"Yes."

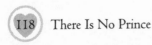

"So what else? Was there anything else he said or did that could have affected your interpretation of his walk?"

"It's not an interpretation, it's the truth," Gemma argued. "It's always been there, and I guess I was just blind to it."

"We'll discuss that in a minute," said Peg. "What else happened?"

"Oh, after we said we loved each other I took off running and challenged him to catch me. He did, and we fell down. We were lying there on the ground when two little boys ran by, and Jules said something about did I want some little hellions when we got married."

"Ah," said Peg, tapping the tip of her pen against her temple. "So he mentioned marriage—and you got scared."

"Scared?" Gemma rolled her eyes. "Please. Why would I be scared?"

"Gemma, when Jules brought up marriage did it frighten you?"

"No," Gemma insisted. "I've always wanted to get married, so why would the mention of it scare me?"

Peg leaned back and looked into Gemma's eyes. "Say, 'I'm scared.'"

Gemma hesitated, looking away.

"Just say it, try it on, see how it feels," urged Peg.

"I'm scared," whispered Gemma.

"Say it again."

"I'm scared," Gemma said, louder. "I'm scared, I'm scared, I'm scared …" Suddenly she was sobbing. "Yes, I am scared. I'm frightened out of my wits. I've finally found the man I want and the relationship I want, and I'm terrified. He wants to marry me!"

"Good, good," murmured Peg as Gemma reached for a tissue from the box beside her chair. "Let yourself feel the fear. And think about how the fear is connected to finding something wrong with the way Jules walks."

Gemma blew her nose decisively. "It's my pitfall. When I'm

afraid a man is getting too close, I get critical. I find something wrong with him and it becomes huge, out of proportion—a fatal flaw."

"Yes! And it used to happen fairly soon after meeting someone, didn't it?" asked Peg.

"Yeah, after a few dates. Like the guy I broke up with because he chewed too loudly." Gemma laughed ruefully.

"So this is amazing, actually," Peg said. "You've gone what, six or seven months without finding a fatal flaw! And it's perfectly natural that it would happen after he brings up the subject of marriage. It's scary to think about commitment, no matter how much you want one. And everyone has their own way of dealing with that fear—it's their own behavioral pitfall. Some women give themselves up, don't acknowledge their fears, and lose themselves in the relationship. You, on the other hand, tend to get overly critical. Now, I want you to imagine why it serves you to get so critical. What purpose is there in it? What does it get you?"

Gemma closed her eyes. "Hmm. I guess it gets me ... space," she said slowly. "If I find something wrong with him, I can distance myself from him. And then I don't have to deal with the scary feelings."

"Very good, Gemma," said Peg. "I think you've really put your finger on it. So what you really need is some distance right now so you can get used to the idea of marrying Jules, is that right?"

"Yes, I guess it is," Gemma agreed.

"So how else can you get space other than obsessing about there being something wrong with him?"

"I guess I could just ask for it," said Gemma. "What a concept!"

Peg smiled. "Yes, what a concept, huh? Asking for what you want. Taking care of yourself. You've been doing a stunning job of it, and now it's just a matter of continuing."

"But what if he gets mad?" asked Gemma. "What if he changes his mind about wanting to be with me?"

"Do you think he will?" asked Peg. "Probably just the opposite, actually. Men like it when you can take care of yourself. And when you are asking for what you desire from a place of loving yourself, you don't have to be fierce about it. You can ask calmly and gently, which will make all the difference. Women tend to get fierce when we don't believe we're worth it, and because we don't feel worthy we go around with our fists out. Or else we give in and turn into a victim, unable to admit we're angry with ourselves for not taking care of ourselves. Do you understand what I mean?"

> *Men like it when you can take care of yourself. When you are asking for what you desire from a place of loving yourself, you don't have to be fierce about it.*

"Yes," said Gemma. "I met Jean at the workshop and she said she always gave herself up in every relationship until she didn't have anything left. And she was angry about it, but she kept acting like a victim and letting men take advantage of her. And I guess I'm kind of the opposite, I get defensive and stick out my fists like you said."

"Exactly. But taking a loving stand for yourself is different," Peg continued. "It means calmly asking for what you want from a strong, centered, openhearted place. Chances are he'll respect that. But if he doesn't want to give you what you're asking for, you'll have to make a decision about it. If he can't handle your taking care of yourself, he may not be the man for you. But I really don't think you have to worry about that with Jules. I'm certain he will allow you all the space and time you need. Just gently reassure him he didn't do anything wrong. Let him know *you* have some work to do."

Gemma nodded, clutching her tissue. It was scary to think of asking Jules for space, but she knew that if she wanted their relationship to continue she'd have to do it. Otherwise, she would keep finding things wrong with him and it would end badly, like all the other relationships she'd had. Thanking Peg, she left her session fearful but resolved. She would call Jules tonight and ask him to come over. She would calmly and quietly ask for what she needed. What *did* she need, exactly? She knew she needed time and distance, but how much?

"I'll mull it over before I see him," she promised herself. "And I can always change my mind."

## Taking a Loving Stand

Jules sat on the overstuffed chair across from Gemma. She handed him a mug of tea, and he set it down on the coffee table, wiping his hands nervously on his corduroys.

"What is it, Gem?" he asked. "I knew something was wrong on our walk yesterday, and when you didn't answer my phone calls I figured you were mad at me."

Gemma smiled at him. "I'm sorry, Jules. I behaved badly, but I'm not mad at you. I realize now that I was scared. I am still scared. You brought up the subject of marriage and kids, and it really freaked me out."

"Oh." Jules looked crestfallen. "God, I feel like an idiot. Was it too soon? I was just in such bliss walking with you, and I thought you felt the same way ..."

"No, I did," Gemma said. "That's probably why I got scared. I've tended to push men away in the past when things got too intense. I'm really working on it, and I don't want to push you away. I love you, and I think I might want to marry you. That's just it, do you see? I'm afraid I'll push you away —and I really don't want to do that."

"Okay," Jules said slowly. "So what do you want?"

Gemma took a deep breath. "I want some time to let all of this sink in. I don't know how much time it will take, but I promise you it will be worth it. I just need some time alone without seeing you for a while. I need to check in with myself, you know?"

"So does this mean you're breaking up with me?" Jules looked down into his mug as if the answer could be found in its depths.

"No, absolutely not," Gemma reassured him. "Like I said, I think I really do want to be with you for the rest of my life. And that is a really overwhelming concept for me. So I need two weeks, or maybe even a month, to let it all sink in. Okay?"

"All right," Jules agreed. "I don't really like it, but if that's what you need, that's what you need. Right? Right. So. I guess I'll go now." He stood up, looking around distractedly for his jacket.

Gemma went to him and put her arms around him. "I love you, and I'll call you when I'm ready," she whispered. She felt a pang as she watched him walk out and close the door. What if he never came back?

"It's up to me," she reminded herself firmly. "I'm doing this for myself. I am taking a loving stand for myself, asking for what I want and getting it. It might not feel great right now, but a good thing is happening." She put her hand on her heart and felt its warmth. "I love you, Gemma," she whispered.

The next three weeks were the hardest Gemma could remember having. She found herself mooning randomly around her apartment, cleaning the same counter over and over again, and staring dejectedly into store windows when she was out. She had a constant internal dialogue going on to help herself through each moment.

"I don't have to be like my mother," she reassured herself over and over. "If I notice I'm starting to give up myself to the relationship the way my mother did, I can help myself. I love myself enough now not to let myself lose the relationship I've gained with myself and my sense of independence."

Sometimes Gemma felt panic seize her. "I was able to take space for myself now, but what if I need space when we're married?"

"Put your hand on your heart and breathe," she would remind herself. When she calmed down, she was able to reassure herself that she would be able to ask for space any time she needed it. Jules loved her and he would understand.

Gemma was so lonely during those weeks that she was tempted to call Jules almost every day, but something inside her wouldn't let her do it. She knew she wasn't ready to talk to him and that if she did, she would only make things worse.

A few days later, Gemma noticed the familiar magnet on her bathroom mirror. "What's the most loving thing I can do for myself now?" Gemma asked her reflection. She realized it had been a while since she'd remembered to ask that. And the minute she asked it, she knew what to do. She grabbed the phone and dialed Jules's number.

A few hours later, Gemma met Jules at their favorite café. As she looked at him, she felt her heart opening so wide it felt like it could encompass the whole world. Jules turned to her and smiled, and Gemma knew everything would be all right.

"So we are together, probably forever," she concluded as she related the story to Peg at their next session. "I feel really ready to make a commitment, and I can tell Jules is, too. It was so huge for me to realize I needed to develop a heartfelt relationship with myself before I could have a good relationship with a man—that I could make myself happy instead of waiting around for a man to make me happy. Once I was happy in my own life, he came along. And because my heart was open, I was able to accept him and the love he gave me."

> *Loving yourself allows you to be loved.*

"Yes, isn't that amazing?" Peg agreed. "When your heart is closed to yourself, it's impossible to take in love. It might be all around you, but you can't receive it. So loving yourself allows you to be loved. Congratulations, Gemma."

### A Rose Is Itself and the Bee Comes: Becoming Irresistible

Swami Satchidananda, a spiritual teacher from India, made the statement, "A rose is itself and the bee comes." When you are

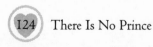

fully yourself and engaged in your life, you attract what you want like a magnet. Falling in love with herself changed the way Gemma related to her own life and altered her magnetism. The same can happen for you when you create a heartfelt relationship with yourself. Like Gemma, when you are in love with yourself, you are irresistible. Your heart is open to yourself and it is open to receiving the love others have to give you.

**When you are fully yourself and engaged in your life, you attract what you want like a magnet.**

When Gemma wasn't loving herself enough, she didn't take care of herself. Inwardly, she was waiting for a Prince to come along to take care of her. Learning to care for herself opened her heart and allowed her to have what she wanted. Like Gemma, many of us think everything will change once we find the right man. Yet it's actually the opposite—once we start nurturing ourselves and taking care of ourselves, *then* we can attract what we want with a man. If you don't have what you want with a man, it's possible that you haven't developed an open-hearted relationship with yourself. You know you haven't been loving yourself enough if you are:

*Thinking there's something wrong with you*
*Not standing up for yourself*
*Choosing the wrong men over and over*
*Allowing yourself to be treated badly*
*Saying yes when you mean no*
*Saying something out of anger that later damages you*
*Criticizing yourself*
*Feeling guilty*
*Having obsessive thoughts*
*Not taking risks*
*Not taking care of yourself physically*
*Not taking care of yourself emotionally*

When you fall in love with yourself, you can:

*Give yourself the time you need to have what you want come into your life.*
*Give yourself gifts and really enjoy them.*
*Decide if something is good for you before doing it.*
*Choose the right man for you.*
*Do what you really want to do instead of what others want you to do.*
*Know that when things aren't going your way, it's not because something is wrong with you.*
*Hold your own hand through the hard parts.*
*Tolerate being lonely rather than being with someone who is not good for you.*
*Set limits with others.*
*Turn your back on what's not good for you.*
*Expect to be treated well.*
*Not take things personally.*
*Believe you are worthy.*
*Accept that you are human.*
*Forgive yourself for making mistakes.*
*Have compassion for your dilemma as a human being on this planet.*
*Be open to receiving the love that is all around you.*
*Have fun.*
*Enjoy your life.*
*Be your own fairy godmother.*

**You can build a practice of loving yourself.**

Like Gemma, you can build a practice of loving yourself. By asking yourself, "What is the most loving thing I can do for myself now?" you will begin to take care of yourself in a new way. You will begin to trust yourself more, know that you can take care of yourself in any situation and be sure that you won't lose yourself in a relationship.

Loving yourself more means you will be able to relax about

life. When you are in a heartfelt relationship with yourself you will be able to trust that you will take care of yourself in the moment. When you are treating yourself lovingly you take a stand for yourself. You will naturally expect to be treated well and get what you need without having to be loud and strident about it. Like Gemma, you will be able to know what you need to do for yourself, and you will be able to ask for it—and have it.

*Like bees to a flower, men are attracted to you when you are blossoming into the fullness of yourself.*

When you are taking a loving stand for yourself, you will:

> *Remember to ask yourself,*
> > *"What is the most loving thing I can do for myself now?"*
> *Trust that you will have the answer*
> *Be treated well*
> *Ask calmly for what you want*
> *Receive it gracefully*

When you are standing strongly at the center of your life you are irresistible. Men want you to be strong, have your own life, and love yourself. When your heart is open and you are living well, people want to be around you. You have an environment of warmth that draws them in. Like bees to a flower, men are attracted to you when you are blossoming into the fullness of yourself.

### Your mother never told you that. . .

*The most important relationship you'll ever have is with yourself.*

*There's nothing wrong with you.*

*It's generous to give yourself good things.*

*Loving yourself is not the same as being selfish.*

When you are in love with yourself, everyone benefits.

You can take care of yourself while in a relationship with a man.

When you love yourself, you'll be able to make good choices.

You can gently ask for what you want.

Doing what is difficult and good for you is self-loving.

When your heart is open to yourself you'll be able to receive the love that is all around you.

When you are in love with yourself, you are irresistible.

## Think about...

 And begin asking "What is the most loving thing I can do for myself now?

The exercises for Chapter Five can be found on page 265.

# CHAPTER SIX

## Feeling Bad So Good Things Can Happen

Shelly had been dating Tim for nearly a year, and Tim had recently moved into her apartment. Since Shelly was used to living alone, this was a big adjustment for her. She had spent a lot of time and money to create a nurturing, uncluttered space where she felt comfortable and serene. When Tim moved in with five suitcases full of clothes, his home theater system, and his La-Z-Boy, it was a challenge for Shelly to accept the changes—even though she was happy to have the closeness she'd always wanted with a man. Because it *was* what she wanted, she worked very hard to be flexible, to allow him his own use of the space, and not to jump on him the second he left a dirty glass in the sink. Yet sometimes the strain of sharing her space grew so great that she couldn't seem to help getting upset.

One morning Shelly got out of bed and as usual shuffled into the kitchen to brew a pot of coffee.

"Oh no, Tim left the old grounds in it again," she groaned to herself. "I've asked him over and over again to clean up after he makes his after-dinner pot of coffee—and every morning it's full of grounds. I have a presentation this morning and I just don't feel like dealing with this today!"

Shelly banged the filter into the garbage and slammed the lid.

"Tim, is it so hard to do this one little thing?" she fumed aloud.

"What?" Tim called sleepily from the bedroom. "Did you say something, honey?"

Shelly walked to the bedroom, holding aloft the dirty coffee pot. "How many times have I asked you to clean the coffee maker after your midnight cup?" she said with an exasperated sigh. "When I'm tired in the morning it's really a drag to be confronted with a dirty coffee pot."

"I'm sorry," said Tim. "I just can't seem to remember to do it. I get going on the Internet and I forget all about it by the time the coffee's gone."

Shelly shook her head. "Well, that's just not good enough, Tim. I mean, I've been trying really hard to be flexible here, but when I've asked you five times nicely I lose my patience!"

Tim pulled the covers over his head. "Mmmph mumble grr," he said.

"What?" Shelly said, brandishing the coffee pot. "I know you just said something. Tell me what it is."

"You sound just like my mother!" Tim said. "It's such a little thing, Shelly, can't you let it go? I mean, what is the big deal?"

"I sound like your mother?" Shelly was furious. "Well maybe you need a mother, Tim. You still leave your socks all over the bedroom floor, you can't seem to remember to put the toilet seat down, and you never, ever help me make the bed. So excuse me if I sound like your mother, but I think she'd agree with me that you need to grow up."

Shelly flounced out of the room, slamming the door behind her. She banged the coffee pot into the sink and stepped into the shower without asking him if he needed to use the bathroom first like she usually did. When she got out he had already left. She was incensed that he would leave without apologizing, and she had an imaginary conversation with him while she pulled on her stockings and did her makeup. By the time she got into her car, she was even angrier than she'd been before. How could Tim blatantly ignore her request to do something so simple? Was it a sign that he'd make a lousy husband and father? Maybe he just didn't care about her enough to consider her needs.

When Shelly arrived at the office, she was in a stew. She stared blankly at the pile of papers on her desk, unable to think about anything except the argument and how inconsiderate Tim had been. She shuffled some papers around, bit the end of her pen until it was ragged, and swiveled her chair around to look out the window.

Suddenly, fear swept through Shelly like a cold wind. Tim was obviously really upset and didn't want to talk to her. It took a lot to upset him, and maybe she had pushed him over the edge this time. Was he considering moving out? Had she messed up their relationship over a stupid coffee pot?

"I've got to call him," Shelly said to herself. "Oh no, he made me promise not to call him at work unless it was an emergency. Last time I called he was very short with me and it made everything worse. But this is an emergency, isn't it? I feel horrible, and I can't stand it another minute. Talking to him *has* to make things better."

Shelly felt her hand creeping toward the phone almost without her volition. She snatched it back, but before she knew it her fingers were dialing his number.

Why was Shelly calling Tim even though she knew it would make the situation worse? Because she couldn't stand how she was feeling. She felt so bad that she was compelled to take action—even though she knew the action might be damaging. We all do this sometimes; in fact, a lot of the choices we make are based on trying not to feel bad. It's natural to want to avoid feeling humiliated, angry, sad, hurt, or afraid. Yet making decisions based on avoiding those feelings is not always in our best interest.

A lot of the choices we make are based on trying not to feel bad.

Sometimes it's important to allow ourselves to feel bad so a good thing can happen.

*Your mother never told you. . .*
    *that sometimes you might have to tolerate feeling bad so a good thing could happen.*

## Phone-in-Hand Disease

When Shelly's fingers crept toward the buttons on the phone—against her better judgment—she was suffering a bout of what we call "phone-in-hand disease." "Phone-in-hand disease" is a peculiar ailment that often begins, as it did for Shelly, when you have an argument with the man in your life in the morning before going to work—or maybe you're still upset about an unresolved argument that happened the night before. As the morning progresses, the feelings you are having get so intense that you can't stand it one more second. You are seized with an almost irresistible urge to call him so you can feel better—or take some other automatic action to try to avoid feeling bad. The problem is, the automatic action doesn't usually make things better. In fact, it tends to have the opposite effect.

The reason it will make things worse to call a man at work is that most men can't talk about emotional issues and concentrate on work at the same time. This is not meant as a criticism, it's just a fact. Men generally don't have the ability to process emotions and get on with their workday at the same time. You might think they ought to be able to do this—because you can do it. But women are programmed to be able to do many things at the same time. Men tend to be a lot more single-minded. It is important to understand that he has a different agenda than you do. His job is very important and when he's there he needs to focus on getting work done. He cannot get his work done and listen to you at the same time.

As a woman, relationship is more central to your life. When a relationship is not going well, it becomes urgent for you to fix it. Your job may be very important to you too, but talking to him doesn't necessarily take away your ability to do your work. In fact, you may need to clear things up in order to get on with your workday. Yet it probably makes him feel very stressed when you try to do that. He needs to win the customer service prize or achieve his sales quota so he can take you on that vacation to the Bahamas. He doesn't know what went wrong, and he wants the argument resolved too—later, when he can focus.

When Shelly dialed Tim's number, she knew on some level that calling him would probably make things worse. Yet on another level, calling him felt like taking care of herself. That's the deceptive nature of "phone-in-hand disease"—or any automatic action you take to try to avoid feeling bad. It seems like you are taking care of yourself by calling him, eating a whole bag of cookies, or going shopping for shoes you can't afford. Yet the end result is that you end up feeling worse.

The only antidote is to allow yourself to feel bad so a good thing can happen. In order to let yourself feel bad, you can go to the bathroom and sit in a stall for a few minutes, take a walk around the block, or close the door to your office. First, let your thoughts go. Then relax your body and focus on your feelings. Being alone with your feelings allows you to feel them—and once you feel them, they move through you and often disappear very quickly. It may be uncomfortable to feel things deeply, yet the intensity of a feeling can last only a few minutes before it subsides. It may not go away completely, but the enormity of it will lessen and you will be able to make a better choice for yourself.

> **Being alone with your feelings allows you to feel them—and once you feel them, they move through you and often disappear very quickly.**

What if Shelly could have tolerated her anger and fear instead of taking an action to try to stop the feelings? Let's say she managed to stop her fingers in mid-dial. She could then remove her hand from the phone, lean back in her chair, and breathe. She could let the feeling *in* through the in-breath and then *out* through the out-breath, slowing her breathing and calming herself down.

Once Shelly let herself feel her feelings, she would be more in touch with herself. She could put her hand on her heart and keep breathing, asking herself what would be good for her to do in that moment. Then she could take an action based on what was good for her rather than on what would stop herself from feeling bad. She could stop herself from reacting only to the immediate problem and take a larger view of the situation. Perhaps she was responding to something in her history. Once she had some perspective, she could create a good future outcome. Instead of acting automatically, she would be making a conscious choice—and she would feel more powerful.

*Your mother never told you...*
  *that feeling your feelings would allow you to*
  *make a better choice for yourself.*

## Building Your Feeling Tolerance

Tolerating your feelings is a muscle that you can develop, just like opening your heart. And it's not a muscle that you have been encouraged to build, because the society we live in is based largely on avoiding feelings. Almost everyone is walking around doing anything they can not to feel bad, without realizing that if they could just feel bad for a while the feeling would pass through them and they could move on. So how can you build your muscle for tolerating feelings? You start by taking it slowly. When you start lifting weights, you start with a two-pound weight first and gradually build weight and repetitions. You can take the same approach with your feelings.

Making the choice to build your tolerance for feeling will change your life. Leaning back, breathing, counting, and quieting the mind all allow you to feel the feeling you are having and let it move through your body. You may need to cry, pound the pillow, scream, or dance around the room to help the feeling move through you. Then don't forget to reward yourself for making a healthy choice. You deserve to have what you want with a man, and you are on your way to having it! And if you are not acting out to avoid feeling bad, your man will be grateful and give you more of what you want.

## Seven Steps to Building Feeling Tolerance

1. *Stop yourself from taking whatever action you feel compelled to take that is not good for you,* such as reaching for the phone.
2. *Lean back and breathe deeply.* Let your feelings come in to your body as you breathe in, and leave your body as you breathe out. Breathing helps you connect with yourself so you will be more likely to do what is good for you.
3. *Quiet the mind.*
   a) *Count to thirty.* Counting helps quiet the mind. Humming is also really useful. Remember when you were a kid and you didn't want to hear something, you would put your hands over your ears and hum or go "lalalalalala" so you wouldn't hear it? It works! Then, if you still need to make the call or take the action, go ahead and do it. At least you have thirty seconds' more perspective now, and you've calmed down a little.
   b) *Count to sixty before taking the damaging action.* Simple, but effective.
   c) *Every time you are in a similar situation, count a little higher before calling or taking the automatic action.* Eventually you will be able to take a considered action that will support you in the long run, and that's better than reacting to the immediate situation.

4. *Get yourself a phone buddy,* a friend who agrees to talk to you when you are about to take an action that is not good for you. If your fingers just have to dial a number, dial your friend first. Speaking to her will help get out some of your feelings. You may still need to call him afterward, but maybe you just needed to talk to somebody. And even if you do call your man afterward, your conversation won't be as charged as it would have been if you hadn't talked to your phone buddy first.

5. *Figure out how you will take care of yourself in a way that is good for you—and do it when the time comes.* Remember to ask yourself, "What is the most loving thing I can do for myself now?"

6. *Be patient with yourself.* Remember, like starting a workout program, building tolerance for your feelings may be hardest at first. The more you do it, the easier it gets.

7. *Congratulate yourself!* You have just accomplished something really big, so celebrate. Make a list of things that are different now that you've built up a muscle. Things to notice could be:

   a) *You feel better about yourself.*

   b) *You feel more in control.*

   c) *You have more power over your thoughts and feelings.*

   d) *You are no longer compelled to take an action that may be damaging to you.*

   e) *You can get through the whole day doing what is good for you.*

   f) *You can soothe yourself when your feelings seem overwhelming.*

   g) *You can creatively experiment with many ways to help yourself when you feel bad.*

   h) *You can have a calmer, more relaxed relationship with yourself and with him.*

*Your mother never told you. . .*
   *that building your tolerance for feelings would
   allow you to make better choices for yourself.*

## Turning Your Back on Old Choices

Making good choices means turning your back on what is not good for you. You are pointing yourself in a new direction, and doing something different from what you've always done. Doing something new can be uncomfortable because it involves entering unknown territory. We naturally prefer what's familiar to what's unknown—even if we are aware that what's familiar won't get us what we want. Turning in a new direction may mean feeling uncomfortable. Yet unlike your familiar discomfort, this discomfort will lessen and eventually disappear.

> *Making good choices means turning your back on what is not good for you.*

Alicia came face-to-face with some uncomfortable feelings two years after taking the Workshop. As she planned her wedding to Lewis, whom she'd met soon after taking our course, she found herself musing on how far she'd come.

"I wonder what the real turning point for me was," Alicia asked herself. "I think it was when I finally turned my back on what wasn't good for me—and was able to choose Lewis with an open heart."

As she started addressing the pile of wedding invitations in front of her, Alicia allowed her mind to wander back through the course of her relationship with her fiancé. She remembered that before taking the Workshop she'd had a pattern of choosing handsome, outgoing, flirtatious men. As she explored her history and beliefs during the course, she discovered that the reason she couldn't resist these men was that they resembled her Uncle Matthew, on whom she'd had a crush throughout her childhood.

Good-looking Uncle Matthew had always been surrounded by a laughing crowd, and the women in the family all adored him. Alicia joined her cousins in vying for his attention, and when he winked at her or sat her on his lap she felt on top of the world.

As an adult, Alicia remained devastatingly attracted to men who were outgoing and who had women falling all over them. When she entered a room, it was the man in the center of a group of giggling women who drew her like a magnet. And it was a challenge for Alicia to get him to notice her above all the others. When he did notice her, she felt valued and successful—and if he asked her out, she was over the moon.

The problem with the excessively gregarious and flirtatious men Alicia chose was that they were unable to commit to just one woman. Alicia would fall for them completely, and then be devastated when they flirted with someone else and eventually ended up leaving her. It wasn't until she'd done a lot of work on herself that she realized she had the choice to select men differently. When she started looking at what she wanted in a man, she understood that the qualities she'd always been drawn to were the opposite of the qualities she really desired.

"What I really want is a man who will always be there for me, who will think I'm the only woman in the world for him, and who will be committed to our relationship one hundred percent," she wrote in her notebook.

Once Alicia had identified what it was she wanted, she was surprised to discover that a man with the very qualities she wanted was already in her life. Yet because he wasn't a gregarious flirt, she hadn't paid him much attention. Lewis, an accountant, always seemed to be hovering on the sidelines. He attended Alicia's parties and went out with her group of friends—yet Alicia had never quite registered him as an eligible man because he was quiet and participated more by watching than by trying to grab the limelight.

Alicia began dating Lewis, who turned out to be attentive, supportive, a good listener, and loyal. In short, Lewis was everything Alicia wanted—yet the very fact that he was always there for her was almost more than she could bear.

"What's wrong with him that he's made me so central in his

life?" she would find herself wondering as she watched him cook dinner for her. "It's like his happiness depends on pleasing me— and that makes me uncomfortable."

Alicia had to work very hard at tolerating her feelings in order to accept the love and devotion Lewis was offering. She had to take a deep breath while she felt the acute discomfort that overtook her when he would call every day, want to spend most evenings with her, listen to everything she said, and show up with tickets for concerts he thought she'd enjoy. Yet because she was committed to making good choices, she knew she had to tolerate feeling bad so a good thing could happen.

After a few months of dating Lewis, Alicia flew to Chicago to attend a conference. The first morning of the event she stepped into the crowded lecture hall and immediately spotted a man talking animatedly to a group of admiring women. Alicia found herself drawn to the group as if hypnotized. Her feet had a life of their own, leading her toward the desirable man seemingly without her volition.

With a huge effort, Alicia stopped her feet from walking into the charmed zone.

"What am I doing, acting on my attraction to a gregarious flirt?" she asked herself. "I must remember that I have the choice not to go near him."

Alicia deliberately sat across the room from the outgoing man, yet she couldn't keep her eyes off him. It was torture to watch him hugging, laughing, and having a great time with all the other women. Alicia didn't hear much of the lecture because she was so preoccupied with stealing glances at him. She couldn't help wondering if he had noticed her or fantasizing that he would approach her after the lecture.

When the lecturer had finished speaking, Alicia took herself firmly in hand and went up to her hotel room. She sat on the bed and breathed deeply, calming her thoughts enough to have a reasonable conversation with herself. "Okay, this is it," she said to herself. "Did you or did you not make a choice to never again get involved with an Uncle Matthew–type?"

"Yes, I did make that choice," she reluctantly admitted to herself.

"And why did you make that choice?" she asked.

"Because in my experience, a man like that will not give me what I want," Alicia answered herself. "And I don't want to go through the anguish and heartbreak anymore. So I have to stay away from the flirtatious men who will end up going away, and turn toward Lewis whom I love and who treats me well."

"Then you are going to have to turn your back on this flirtatious man at the conference," she warned. "Congratulations—you did a great job of not approaching him when you walked into the lecture hall. You noticed what you were doing, woke up, and turned away. Now when you go to lunch I want you to choose a nice woman to sit next to. And I want you to go through the entire weekend without approaching him."

Alicia managed to get through the weekend without breaking her promise to herself, but it took all her energy and strength. Even though she knew that getting involved with an Uncle Matthew–type would be bad for her, it felt so awful to resist it that she nearly gave in several times. Yet she knew that the only way toward happiness was to tear herself away from her old habits and stick by her new choices, so Alicia managed to get through the weekend without giving in.

When she arrived home, Alicia dropped her bags and rushed to the answering machine. The light was blinking rapidly, and there were three messages from Lewis telling her how much he missed her. Listening to them filled her with joy and relief. She had done it—she had resisted what she had always done and had made a different choice! And now she had the chance to have a relationship that might truly make her happy.

When she told her story at the next Relationship Support Group at Life Works, the women all cheered and applauded. They knew how difficult it was for Alicia to turn her back on the gregarious man and make a different choice. After the meeting, Norma came up to Alicia and clasped her hand.

"Alicia, your story really inspired me," she said. "I've been trying to give up my current boyfriend who I know isn't good for me, and now I'm thinking maybe I really can do it. So thanks."

Alicia felt her heart swell. She knew that from then on she would be able to appreciate Lewis in a new way and give herself wholeheartedly to their relationship. It wouldn't always be easy, but she knew her perception had shifted enough to keep her facing in a healthy direction. Because she'd turned her back on her old choices, she could now trust herself to take action based on what was good for her rather than what felt comfortable and familiar.

Alicia addressed the last wedding invitation with a flourish.

"Yes, that conference was the turning point," she thought. "It's not like things were always easy after that. I still have to deal with discomfort. It's still not easy for me to risk hurting his feelings when I need to ask for more distance or do something to take care of myself. Yet Lewis knows now that I've fallen more deeply in love with him and that asking for what I need continues to allow me to love him more fully.

"I'm going to spend the rest of my life with Lewis, and there will be times when I still crave that Uncle Matthew–type. Yet now I know I can live through it and come out the other side with a larger understanding, more compassion for myself, a stronger commitment to changing my life for the better—and trusting that I can count on myself to make good choices."

*Your mother never told you...*
*that making new choices means turning your*
*back on what's not good for you.*

*Think about...*

 Times you turned your back on what wasn't good for you so you could have what you want.

*The exercises for Chapter Six can be found on page 266.*

# CHAPTER SEVEN

# *Having Your Future Be Different From the Past*

"I met this guy at a party last night and I think he's The One," announced Angela dramatically. Jeanette sighed. "Did you hear me, Jeanette?" Angela asked.

"Yes," Jeanette said without enthusiasm. "You met The One."

"Well, you don't seem very happy for me," Angela pouted.

Jeanette hesitated, then decided to be honest. Since taking Relationship Course she had been biting her tongue, but she just couldn't sit back and watch Angela shoot herself in the foot again.

"It's just that you've been through all this before, hon," she said. "You see a man across a crowded room, the theme from *Love Story* starts playing in your head, and suddenly you are swept into a romance almost without your volition. It feels like fate, destiny ... something larger than yourself is pulling you toward him. Your knees get wobbly, you can't think of a single coherent sentence, and you are suddenly sure you have a piece of spinach caught between your teeth. He's the Prince—you're sure of it, and the outcome is beyond your control. Right?"

Angela was silent. "I'm sorry if I sounded a little harsh, Angela," said Jeanette gently. "It's just that I don't want to watch you go through this again."

"Go through what, exactly?" Angela's voice tightened a bit. "What makes you think it won't be different this time?"

We all tend to think that meeting Mr. Right is a matter of chance or fate. He comes into our lives, he looks like the Prince we've been promised, we feel a physical attraction, and if he feels it too, we figure he must be The One.

The problem is, when we leave finding our man up to chance or fate, we feel powerless. We attract who we attract, and then we have to try to make it work. And because we each have our own history and beliefs about life, we keep attracting the same kind of man.

Angela's friend Jeanette used to end up with men who lived out of town. It wasn't until she really looked at the whole picture of her relationships with men in our workshop, though, that she realized her behavior was a pattern. Jeanette just thought she was unlucky in love. When she started to see the pattern, she understood that having long-distance relationships kept her from having to get too intimate. And that was her comfort zone. But at the same time she wanted to get married, and she couldn't understand why that wasn't happening.

There's nothing wrong with having a pattern. We attract what we expect based on our history—it's unavoidable. But if you're not *aware* that you have a pattern, that's where there's a problem. Because you don't see that you have choices. You don't understand that you are selecting men unconsciously based on what you learned growing up. And that might not be the best way of selecting for yourself.

When considering your patterns, pay special attention to physical appearance. It is amazing how much our selection of a man is based on it. How many times have you looked at someone and dismissed him because he's not your type? And you probably never stopped to wonder *why* the men you liked *were* your type. Why do some women date only men over six feet tall, and some women date only men with brown hair and blue eyes? The physical attributes that attract you are usually based on your history. Maybe, for example, you spent hours watching your father build model airplanes, so you have a visual memory of his delicate hands. And you're automatically attracted to men with similar hands.

In Chapter Two we told the story of Sharon, a woman who had done a lot of work on herself. Yet she was still having trouble with relationships with men. When she did some more exploration into her history, the woman realized that for thirty years she'd been selecting men based on the fact that they had red hair—without realizing it. She was selecting men based on an unconscious expectation that red hair meant they were like her uncle, who had red hair and whom she looked up to as a model for being a desirable man. So she unconsciously saw every red-haired man as someone who was ambitious, successful, and could support her financially.

Your pattern is not always so blatant, of course, but a lot of times it is. And it's not only physical characteristics. We choose men based on aspects of their personality in the same way. We choose men who have issues or problems that will stimulate feelings and situations that are familiar to us. In this chapter, you will begin to recognize your own patterns of selection—and to learn what you can do to choose and attract a man who is authentically good for you into your life.

*Your mother never told you. . .*
*that you have conscious and unconscious patterns of selection.*

## Your Patterns of Selection

Have you ever wondered, "Why does this keep happening to me? Why do I keep getting my heart broken?" You may have been unaware that you are attracted to (and therefore choosing) men based on certain characteristics that feel familiar to you. You may not have even been aware that you were making a choice, because it seemed like the attraction just *happened* to you.

❧

**When we become aware of our patterns of selection, we can change the type of men we get involved with.**

❧

Who we end up with is no accident of fate or luck. We have the power to draw certain people toward us. When we become aware of our patterns of selection, we can change the type of men we get involved with. Instead of falling into relationship with the first man you're attracted to, you can take time to make a selection that will be good for you.

Taking your time means loving yourself enough to know there will be another man out there who will be interested in you. You don't have to say yes to the first man who asks you to go away for the weekend. Men want women—they always have and they always will. When you are loving yourself and nurturing your relationship with yourself, you will give yourself the time you need to select a good partner.

Once you begin looking at your patterns of selection you may be amazed at how blatant some of your patterns are and stunned that you haven't noticed them before. You also probably didn't

❧

**When you are loving yourself and nurturing your relationship with yourself, you will give yourself the time you need to select a good partner.**

❧

know that you could change them if you wanted to. You may have been missing out on a lot of great men simply because their physical appearance didn't fit into your puzzle. The woman who loved redheads passed up quite a few men in the thirty years she was selecting partners based on hair color. Realizing she could be attracted to men with brown, black, or blond hair opened up a new world for her. And it allowed her to start looking for the qualities that would make a good husband for her, no matter what his hair color.

What is *your* pattern? It may consist of more than one of the traits listed below, or it may contain one we haven't listed. We created the following list to get you thinking. See what resonates:

*Men who are unavailable*
*Men who get serious right away*
*Men who need to be saved*
*Men who are too old for you*
*Men who don't live up to their potential*
*Men who are immature*
*Men who are insecure*
*Men who have beards*
*Men who are clean-cut*
*Men who do not want children*
*Men who want you to have children*
*Men who can't commit*
*Men who are arrogant*
*Men who are rich*
*Men who get more attached to you than you are to them*
*Men who are self-centered*
*Men who are under-earners*
*Men with broad shoulders*
*Men who are angry at women*
*Men who are uncommunicative*
*Men who are jokesters*
*Men who are confronting*
*Men who are tall*
*Men who are critical*
*Men from different cultures*
*Men who are unwilling to participate with you*
*Men who are artists*
*Men who live far away*
*Men who have flared nostrils*
*Men who are "wimps"*

*Men who are "macho"*

*Men who are stingy*

*Men who show their affection by giving you presents*

*Men who work with their hands*

*Men who don't get along with their mothers*

*Men who love their mothers more than any other woman*

*Men who wear suits*

*Men who only wear jeans and t-shirts*

Some patterns of selection are easier to see than others, but it is certain that you have them. Even if you choose men who seem very different from each other, look deeply and you will discover that there is something about each one that is the same. If it's something that is good for you—your pattern is to go for men who are intelligent, men who are financially stable, or men who are fun-loving—that's a pattern you might want to keep. But if it's something that keeps you frustrated and disappointed in relationship, it's something you will want to change. And you have the power to change what you attract.

**You have the power to change what you attract.**

It's easy to underestimate your power to attract what you choose. It's easy to settle for something that is less than what you want and deserve. Yet you are worth the time it takes to select a man who will give you what you *want* instead of a man who will give you what you *expect*. You don't have to get six months into a relationship and ask yourself, "How did I end up with this guy?"

*Your mother never told you...*
*that you have the power to select a man who is good for you.*

## It Just Keeps Happening...

Phoebe and her two sisters adored their father. He was tall and dignified, always dressed impeccably, and seemed to know everything. He had an important job at a bank, and he arrived home every evening precisely at five-thirty. The girls would line up at the front window, excitedly watching for his sleek gray car to pull into the driveway. Then they would rush to the door and hug him as he set down his shiny briefcase.

When he had managed to pry the girls' arms away from him, Phoebe's father would scoop up Becky, the youngest, and toss her in the air as she squealed in delight.

"How's my little beanie?" he'd ask, setting her down and ruffling her red curls. "Tell me the new word you learned for me today, won't you?"

In her adorable lisp, Becky would proudly shout the word of the day. Their father would laugh in delight and produce a piece of candy from his pocket.

"There you go, beanie. Save it for after dinner," he would admonish as Becky solemnly put the reward in the pocket of her pinafore.

Next, their father would lean down and look gravely into the eyes of Ruth, the oldest.

"Ruth, I hope you got a good grade on the history test I helped you study for," he would say.

Ruth would always glow with pride, nodding her head so vigorously her auburn braids bounced.

"Oh yes, Daddy, I got an A minus on my history test. I'm sorry I didn't get an A, but it was really hard."

"Great work, Ruth," their father would say. "I always knew you were the brains of the family. Keep it up and you'll win the Nobel Prize someday." Then he would plant a kiss on the top of her head and yank her braid affectionately.

Phoebe, the middle sister, was always the last one her father spoke to. She would stand there watching him, longing for his attention as he focused on her other sisters. When he finally turned to her, her heart would leap hopefully. But the most he ever said was, "Well, Phoebe, behaving yourself?"

Phoebe wanted desperately to say something smart or cute, but she could never think of anything. Tongue-tied, she would just nod, looking down at her scuffed brown shoes. Her father would hesitate, and sometimes he would pat her absently on the head. But he would reach for his briefcase immediately, saying, "Well girls, I'm going to go upstairs and take off this monkey suit," heading wearily up the wide staircase.

Many years and many heartbreaks later, Phoebe realized how much her unsatisfied longings for her father's attention had affected her relationships with men.

"I was happy most of the time, but there was one thing that really bothered me," she told Carole, her Guidess. "Since I was the middle sister, I could never seem to get my father's attention the way I wanted to. My older sister Ruth got a lot of attention because she was the smart one, and my younger sister Becky got a lot of attention because she was the baby. My father was always kind to me, but I never felt he cared about me as much as he cared about my other sisters."

"What made you think he didn't care about you as much as he did about them?" Carole asked.

"Well, he always seemed to notice me sort of vaguely, as if I were slightly out of focus. Don't get me wrong, he wasn't deliberately cruel to me or anything. He was always perfectly pleasant. But he wasn't particularly warm with me, and it seemed like he preferred interacting with Ruth and Becky."

"That must have been painful," said Carole sympathetically. "How did you deal with the pain back then?"

Phoebe thought for a while. "I guess I just learned to avoid the pain by expecting that he would pay more attention to Ruth and Becky. I think unconsciously I must have decided that if I *expected* to come last in my father's affections, it wouldn't hurt as much."

"Mm-hmm," Carole said, nodding. "That was a sensible decision at the time—but like most of the expectations we form to protect ourselves, it didn't work in the long run, right?"

"Right," agreed Phoebe. "Because now that I'm an adult, I still expect to come last in a man's affections."

Since we get what we expect in relationships, we can see that Phoebe had formed a belief—a belief that the men she became involved with wouldn't put her first When Phoebe noticed her pattern, she saw that the men in her life always had other attachments that took priority over their relationship with her.

Phoebe had had three long-term relationships with men who were kind to her and treated her well. Yet she always found herself wanting more intimacy than they could give her, and she was frustrated. They wouldn't spend enough time with her, cuddle with her as much as she wanted, or tell her they loved her. After a while the relationship would wind down and the men would just drift away. And in every case, she would hear later that they had gotten seriously involved with someone else quite soon. Two of her ex-boyfriends even ended up marrying the woman they met just after Phoebe.

While working with her Guidess, Phoebe realized that she had something to do with the men she was attracting. She saw that her belief that a man wouldn't put her first kept her in a pattern of attracting men who treated her kindly and distantly like her father did—and who preferred other women to her like she thought her father did.

As Phoebe explored, she saw she was always shy and awkward around her father—and that she got the same way around men. She would hang back, and not reveal too much of herself. "The funny thing is," she told her Guidess, "I'm quite entertaining when I'm around my girlfriends. But around men I just clam up— even when I've known them for a long time. I guess I'm probably not too exciting to be around because I'm so self-conscious. It's like I'm always observing myself from a distance. That ability is very helpful in my writing career, but not so helpful in relationship. Since I maintain this reserved distance, I guess eventually the men go for someone more open and dynamic."

For Phoebe, as for all of us, awareness was the key. When she realized why all her relationships had ended the way they did, she was able to shift her belief that men would not put her first. She became more of her authentic, involved, entertaining self around men. And she was on her way to creating a life that was more authentic and good for her.

*Your mother never told you...*
*that you would develop patterns based on your beliefs.*

## Your Patterns of Belief

Patterns of belief are so ingrained that we often don't realize they're something we learned, not an absolute truth. Even if people all around us are having different experiences than we are, we have blinders on that don't allow us to see that our patterns of belief could change. While Phoebe was being left by men over and over, she had friends who were getting married and staying married. Her friends were cherished and a central part of their men's lives—but Phoebe didn't see that it was possible that she too could have a man who would prefer her over anyone else. That's how strongly our patterns of belief rule our lives.

When you identify your beliefs, you are 90 percent of the way to changing them. When Phoebe became aware of her pattern, she was able to shift it by taking the following steps:

### Shifting a pattern
1. *Get clear about what you want (see chapter 12).*
2. *Take it slow when you are dating someone. Ask a lot of questions and get to know him better before getting involved.*

3. *Create a new belief.* Phoebe created the belief, "Men find me dynamic and interesting." This belief allowed her to be more outgoing around the men she dated. She spoke up more and shared her witty observations instead of keeping them inside.
4. *If you notice that the man you are dating fits your old unhealthy pattern, stop seeing him.*
5. *Tolerate your feelings of sadness and fear when you stop seeing him, and trust that there will be another man coming along who will fit your new belief.*
6. *Put your energy toward uncovering hidden conversations, healing your past, and loving yourself more so you can start attracting a man who's good for you.*

Phoebe was able to change the shape of her puzzle piece once she knew she'd been choosing men who fit into her pattern. Seeing that she was living out her history helped her understand there was nothing wrong with her. Loving herself more allowed her to heal the pain of her father's indifference and move toward someone she would allow to cherish her.

### Examples of patterns of belief:

**Belief:** "I will never be chosen when competing for the attention of a man."

*Possible patterns: She withdraws from competition.*
*She tries too hard and drives men away.*
*She walks away even if the man is interested.*

**Belief:** "I'll never get what I want."

*Possible patterns: She chooses men who do not give to women.*
*She doesn't stay around long enough to get what she wants.*
*She's overly critical and unpleasant.*

**Belief:** "I'm not beautiful and only beautiful women attract handsome men."

*Possible patterns: She dates unattractive men and is always dissatisfied with them.*
*She always criticizes herself out loud.*
*She doesn't present herself well.*

**Belief:** "A good man is hard to find."

**Possible patterns:** *She finds only bad men.*

*The good men she meets are all married.*

*She doesn't notice the good things about the men she meets.*

**Belief:** "A relationship with conflict is more exciting."

**Possible patterns:** *She ends up with men who are jealous and possessive.*

*She chooses men whose behavior is unpredictable.*

*She finds men who are competitive and enjoy arguing.*

*Your mother never told you. . .*
*that you could shift your patterns of belief.*

### Could It Have *Something* to Do With You?

Holly couldn't seem to stay in a relationship with a man for more than a few months. But when she met Richard, a successful entrepreneur with a great sense of humor, she thought things would be different. After going out on several dates with him, she discovered that he wanted to get married and have a family. Holly was thrilled with Richard's romantic overtures and his openness. He took her to the ballet and for drives through the countryside, and he made no secret of the fact that he was very serious about their relationship. He wanted three children just like Holly did, and they agreed they were both ready to start a family.

After Holly had been seeing Richard for nearly six months, she noticed he was always a little late for their dates. He started keeping her waiting longer and longer every time, and twice he canceled at the last minute. Holly was hurt and confused.

"What's going on, Richard?" she finally asked after he'd canceled the second time. "Is there something I've done that's offended you?"

Richard looked surprised. "No, not at all. Everything's fine."

"Then why are you getting later and later every time we have a date, and why are you suddenly starting to cancel on me?" Holly asked.

"I've just gotten really busy at work lately," Richard explained. "It will get better, I promise. I'm just slammed right now."

Holly accepted Richard's explanation, but things didn't get better. His lateness continued and he seemed to get so busy that they were spending less and less time together. It was obvious to her that Richard's ardor had cooled. She found herself getting impatient with waiting for him, and when they were together she couldn't help snapping at him sometimes or picking a fight about some small thing. Richard seemed surprised when she expressed dissatisfaction with the way things were going, insisting everything was fine. They seemed to be at an impasse.

Holly couldn't understand why things had suddenly taken a downward turn. She went to see Gloria, a Life Works Guidess, about it.

"I thought he was different, but he's just like every other man I've been with," she explained despairingly. "When it hits the six-month mark they start acting weird, and eventually they just drop off the face of the earth. They just can't face having to commit."

"So you've noticed that your relationships start to go bad after six months?" Gloria asked.

Holly thought about it for a minute. "Yes, actually," she said. "Just about every relationship I've had has started to get very rocky at six months. He's met someone else, or he just starts to drift away. Hmm ... do you think that has some significance?"

"I think it must," Gloria said. "It seems like a pretty clear-cut pattern, and usually when it's that clear-cut it's because of an anniversary."

"An anniversary?" Holly asked, puzzled. "I wish I had an anniversary to celebrate, but I don't!"

"Not a wedding anniversary," Gloria said, smiling. "An anniversary of something that happened to you at a certain age. Often we unconsciously relive a bad experience when a relationship reaches the number of months or years that correspond to when the original event happened."

"I'm not sure I understand," Holly said.

"Say something traumatic happened to you when you were three and a half years old. You might find later in life that your relationships all went bad after three and a half months or three and a half years," explained Gloria.

"Really?" Holly was taken aback. "That seems so … obvious, I guess, but I never thought about it before."

"It's really amazing how powerfully the unconscious responds to anniversaries," Gloria said. "Didn't you tell me you were six years old when your parents got divorced and your dad moved to California?"

"Yes, I was in first grade so I must have been six," said Holly. She shook her head. "It's too much of a coincidence that all my relationships end at six months."

"It's no coincidence," Gloria replied. "Trust me, your unconscious is remembering what happens and starts making trouble six months in. If you could stay with someone through it, you might find you have trouble again at six years. It's amazing, but that's how the unconscious works."

Holly was indignant. "So it's *my* fault things start to go bad at six months? But *they're* the ones who start acting strange, not me."

"I'm not saying you're doing something consciously. But you're the one who's in every one of your relationships that end after six months," Gloria said gently. "So something in your unconscious is seeing trouble at the six-month mark. It sounds to me like you are reacting to the pain of your parents' divorce when you were six, and you're expecting the man to leave because that's what your father did."

Holly let this new information sink in. The more she thought about it, the more she realized it must be true.

"So I'm living out a pattern of behavior that has my relationships go sour at six months," she mused.

"It sure looks that way," said Gloria. "And when you can own your part in the pattern, you'll have the power to change it."

Gloria gave Holly the assignment to go back over her past relationships in the light of remembering her parents' divorce at age six. At home, as he sat with her notebook, she pictured her past relationships as if they were rolling past her on a movie screen. She saw that because she'd been living in anticipation that a man would leave, she had been reliving her parents' divorce by becoming increasingly angry and irrational.

*Seeing your part in the pattern means that you can stay awake next time, and you'll have the power to change the outcome.*

"I start criticizing him and closing in on him," Holly said to herself. "I'm so afraid he'll leave that I start nagging him, and that ends up pushing him away. Then he leaves me, and it looks like that's the reason for the breakup—when in fact I forced him into a corner."

Holly was overcome with sadness as she realized how powerfully she'd been sabotaging her relationships. Of course the men had played their part, but she'd never seriously considered that she had a pattern of pushing men away. "It's perfectly natural to be sad for what has happened in the past," said Gloria. "But now you know it can be different next time. Seeing your part in the pattern means that you can stay awake next time, and you'll have the power to change the outcome."

*Your mother never told you...*
  *that owning your part in a pattern would give you the power to have it be different next time.*

## Your Patterns of Behavior

Like Holly, you have anniversaries of important or traumatic events that keep cropping up in your life. Yet if you don't know to look for the pattern, you might never recognize it and instead blame the man or the circumstances when something goes wrong. It can be very illuminating to look at past relationships or dating patterns as Holly did. You can notice when trouble started and clearly see your part in the situation.

> You can make a different choice than the one you've always made. And you will get a different result.

For example, if you never get past the third month in a relationship, it may well be that you have unresolved issues with a sibling being born into the family when you were three. When you are aware of the anniversary, you can prepare yourself for it and be extra awake when the date comes around. Even if you still have trouble around that time, at least you will know why it is happening. You won't blame your man or the circumstances, and you will have a basis for dealing with the situation without blame. Blaming men or blaming circumstances keeps you powerless. When you start seeing your patterns of behavior you have the opportunity to change them.

It's important to notice and admit to yourself that you have ways of behaving and reacting in relationship that are the same every time. It may look to you like the circumstances are different, but when you start examining your past relationships you can start to see the patterns. It may seem like things are just happening to you, but actually you are creating what happens—often unconsciously.

**Patterns of behavior can include:**
> *How much you can tolerate loneliness*
> *How frequently you go out on dates*
> *How fast you get into a serious relationship*
> *How long your relationships last*
> *How critical you are*
> *How well you let him get to know you*
> *How soon the relationship gets physically intimate*

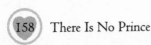

*How trusting you are*
*How jealous you are*
*How busy you are*
*How much you leave your own life behind*
*How easily you lose interest*
*How long you hang on even though you know it's over*

When you become aware of a pattern of behavior, it helps you know what to watch for. Everyone has different red flags they need to be aware of when things get difficult. Seeing the part you play in the pattern gives you the power to have it be different next time.

Doing something different from the way you've always done it means becoming aware of the patterns you've been living from and identifying the ones that don't work for you. When you can see a pattern, you have the power to stop yourself from repeating it. You can make a different choice than the one you've always made. And you will get a different result.

**To identify a pattern you can ask yourself:**
*What keeps happening?*

**To see what keeps happening, you can look at:**
*The type of men you attract*
*The kind of relationship you find yourself in over and over again*
*The way you behave in relationships*
*The way men behave in relationship to you*
*What keeps happening that upsets you*
*How your relationships end*

When you are aware of your patterns, you will know what to watch for as you meet new men and begin new relationships. If you want your relationships to be different than they have been in the past, it will help to keep your patterns in mind when you start getting involved with someone.

*Your mother never told you...*
  *that you've developed patterns that determine*
  *who and what you attract into your life.*

## Changing a Pattern

Identifying your patterns gives you the power to change what is in your life. When you see that you are about to repeat a pattern you will be able to ask yourself, "Do I want to do it differently this time?" The answer to that question might not always be yes. There are things you have been doing over and over that are good for you, and you will want to keep doing those things. What you will want to change are the patterns that are keeping you from being happy. Examine your patterns closely. Are some of them keeping you comfortable? You developed patterns early in life to keep you feeling safe, but what is safe and comfortable is not necessarily what is good for you. Phoebe felt comfortable maintaining an emotional distance from men and not revealing too much of herself—yet her reserve kept men from getting close to her, and they eventually drifted toward someone else.

> **Identifying your patterns gives you the power to change what is in your life.**

> **It's worth risking the unknown to have the relationship you want.**

Becoming aware of a pattern is an important step, yet knowing about it doesn't necessarily mean a pattern will change. Because they are learned and repeated from an early age, our patterns are ingrained. You tend to move toward your patterns as if magnetized, even when you are working hard on yourself. Patterns keep you feeling safe because when you're repeating what you've always done, you know what to expect. If you change what you do, you don't know what will happen. Change is risky. Yet it's worth risking the unknown to have the relationship you want.

There are a few steps you can take to ensure your patterns will be able to shift:

1. *Look over your history of selecting and interacting with men so you become aware of the patterns you've been repeating.*
2. *Ask your best, most supportive friends what patterns they notice in you. Often it is easier for someone else to see your patterns than for you to see them.*
3. *Identify what had you develop that pattern.*
   *Was it something that happened in your history?*
   *Does it stem from a belief you hold?*
   *Is it what happens in your family?*
   *Does it have to do with not loving yourself?*
   *Expect that your unconscious will reveal the answer in its own time, perhaps when you are not searching for it.*
4. *Look to see how the pattern actually keeps you feeling safe, comfortable, and in familiar circumstances.*
5. *Decide what you would like to shift—whether it's a way of selecting men, a belief you're holding, or a way of behaving.*
6. *Be willing to tolerate a level of discomfort as you begin to do things differently, knowing that as you adjust to a new pattern it will get more comfortable.*

Patterns may not change right away. It takes time to make a shift in how you've always done things. You may find yourself repeating a pattern even though you are working on shifting it. When you catch yourself, you can simply say, "Ah, here I am repeating that pattern!" As you adjust to doing things differently, you will be able to catch yourself sooner and sooner until eventually you will notice that you have actually shifted the pattern. When you start attracting different men and different circumstances that are closer to what you want, you will know your pattern has shifted. Instead of just settling for what has always happened, you will see that you have the power to attract a relationship that will be good for you and right for you.

*Your mother never told you...*
*that you have the power to act and react differ-*
*ently than you have always done.*

*Think about...*

 **Your patterns of selection, belief, and behavior.**

*The exercises for Chapter Seven can be found on page 267.*

# CHAPTER EIGHT

# Owning Your Part

Sheryl sat in the teachers' lounge eating her salad and half-listening to Marge talk about the argument she had with her husband the night before.

"*I* created this lunchtime sharing circle," Sheryl thought, crunching on a stalk of celery. "Before, all the teachers sat in small clusters talking among themselves about their new hairdos. Now they sit in a circle and share the important issues in their lives."

The teachers burst into laughter and Sheryl smiled, still immersed in her thoughts.

"I instigated group hugs in all my first grade classes and encouraged the kids to share their feelings with each other. All my friends and family come to me for comfort and sympathetic advice. I'm known around here as the 'Queen of Intimacy.'"

Sheryl took a sip of her iced tea. "So why can't I have an intimate relationship with a man?"

A month and a half later, Sheryl was discussing her dilemma during a "paired share" at the "Having What You Want With a Man" Workshop.

"I realized something was wrong one night a couple of months ago as I was watching TV with my then-boyfriend Steve," Sheryl began. "He was really into the football game and I wanted to cuddle. I kept trying to get between him and the television, and he was getting more and more annoyed. Finally he snapped at me.

'Sheryl, you're always reaching for me and clinging to me. It drives me crazy!'

"I was so hurt that I left his apartment and walked the two miles home. But along the way, I realized Steve was right. I always seemed to want more intimacy than a man could give me. It was as if I was constantly in a leaning forward position, reaching out to him—and he was constantly pulling back. The more I thought about it, the more I realized it was true. It had been that way with every man I'd ever dated.

"I came to this Workshop to find out why I always end up with men who don't want to be as intimate as I do. I'm tired of ending up feeling rejected and wondering what's wrong with me that he doesn't want to see me more than once or twice a week.

"Basically, I want to have a close, committed relationship with a man—and I need to find out why I can't have one." Stating her dilemma aloud gave Sheryl a feeling of relief. She began to have hope that things could change for the better.

"In this Workshop I uncovered a hidden conversation about closeness. I began to understand that the reason I attract distant men is that I need distance. And that's shocking to me. I thought I wanted nothing more than commitment, devotion, and attention.

"But I can see now it was other people who were actually doing the sharing. I was always the listener, the leader, the facilitator —and I rarely shared anything personal with anyone. I wouldn't let anyone get to know me too well and I was very protective about my personal space. In fact, it's a big deal for me to be sharing my intimate revelations with this group right now—that's why I felt I needed to do it."

Sheryl took a deep breath and sank back into her chair. She could feel sweat trickling down the back of her neck from the tension of sharing with over forty people she had just met that morning. Now that she'd done it, she felt strangely peaceful and calm.

In the days following the Workshop, Sheryl continued to uncover ever-deeper layers of her intimacy issues. She realized it had taken her thirty-two years to own her need for distance because it shattered her carefully constructed identity. Choosing distant men meant that Sheryl could have space without having to disrupt her ideas about who she was. Yet this came at a great cost because she was never in charge of when she saw him and she always ended up feeling abandoned and rejected.

"I could have a man who wanted intimacy as much as or more than I do because I can be the one to call the shots," she wrote in her journal. "If I feel him getting too close, I could be the one to ask for space. What a concept! Instead of being in a leaning forward position grasping for his attention, I could be the one to pull back. Then instead of feeling rejected and powerless, I could feel empowered and be taking care of myself."

When Cynthia took the Workshop, she was surprised to learn she had a silent committee member who emphatically did not want anyone to get too close. She only felt safe when there was a certain amount of physical and emotional distance between her and the people around her. And it didn't take her long to connect her committee member's need for distance with her mother's overly protective and smothering love.

Cynthia remembered how when she was a child her mother would say to her, "It's freezing in here. Go put on a sweater."

"But I'm not cold," Cynthia would protest.

"How could you not be cold? It can't be over fifty degrees," her mother would reply. "You're cold. Go get yourself a sweater." And Cynthia would troop to her room to get a sweater, feeling angry and confused. She knew she wasn't cold, but her mother told her she was cold and her mother must be right.

Now Cynthia realized it was her mother who was cold—but since she didn't have any boundaries between herself and her daughter, she couldn't separate her own chill from Cynthia's physical experience. Even though Cynthia heard that lots of mothers made the irritating sweater comment, Cynthia felt that it was an important example of the way her mother didn't see her as a separate being and often treated her as an appendage of herself. Cynthia felt it was important for her to share her discovery during the course.

"I have a committee member who's been silently keeping people at a distance because when I was a child, it felt to me like my mother lived under my skin," Cynthia went on. "Closeness meant being totally smothered and unable to get out from her influence. I couldn't even trust my own body sensations to tell me if I was cold or not. So I avoided closeness, yet I also wanted it. Later, I cultivated a way to be close without letting anyone under my skin. That way, I was protected from anyone intruding into my space, overpowering me, and making me feel confused like my mother did."

## Being Powerful

It was exhilarating for Krista to think that she could take back her power in relationship, yet it was also very uncomfortable. She decided to join the Life Works Relationship Support Group to help herself make important shifts in her life.

"I know that if I want to have an intimate relationship, I have to be willing to ask for space without feeling guilty," she said to the Group at her first meeting. "I'm used to having a lot of time to myself to work on my art projects—time I used to wish I was spending with a man, but which I now realize is essential for my well-being. Now I can *choose* to spend the time by myself rather than feeling like I'm just filling up space until I can see my man again." Sharing her discomfort helped Krista know that she would be able to take care of herself in a new way when the next man came into her life.

One day, it happened—she met the man she'd always wanted. Gene was attentive, communicative, in touch with his feelings, and open about his desire for a commitment. After their first date, Krista knew that this would be different from any of her previous relationships—and after two weeks, she knew without a doubt that she wanted to marry Gene. He loved having long, intimate conversations and cuddling for hours. He planned nights out on the town and days at museums and shops. Krista was blissfully happy. Here was the closeness she'd wanted all along!

After a couple of months, though, Krista realized she was uncomfortable with the amount of time Gene wanted to spend with her.

"He wants to see me every evening," she said at her Relationship Support Group. "And lately he's been bringing me travel brochures—he wants us to go to Europe together. Suddenly it all feels like too much. I'm getting the urge to run away. I can't even be as nice to him as I want to be because I feel like I have to keep him at arm's length."

"What can you do to support yourself so you don't have to run away?" asked Maureen.

"Well, I could ask for space—a few nights to myself, maybe," said Krista. "I know that. But ..." She shook her head.

"What's holding you back?" Maureen prompted.

"I'm afraid," Krista said. "I've never asked a man for space before, and I'm afraid it will hurt him. I know what it feels like to be the one being pushed away. It makes me feel guilty."

"And what will happen if you hurt him?"

"He'll stop loving me," said Krista immediately, and then recoiled in surprise. "Wow, I didn't even know I was thinking that."

"That's a good realization," Maureen said encouragingly. "Why do you think you might believe he'll stop loving you if you ask for space?"

"I guess because my mother never accepted my talents and interests," said Krista slowly. "She expected me to help with the younger ones and would lay a guilt trip on me if I wanted to paint or draw."

"Mmm," Maureen said, nodding sympathetically. "So you have a committee member who thinks Gene will do what your mother did."

"Yes, it sure looks that way," said Krista.

"Did you ever stop loving a man because he was pushing you away?" asked Maureen.

"No," Krista admitted. "It made me want him more, actually. But it's so scary to be on the other end and not know how Gene will react. Still, it helps to know that it's my mother I'm responding to—not the man I love."

That night, Krista sat on the sofa with Gene and gently explained her dilemma.

"I'm afraid you'll go away completely if I ask for some space," she confessed. "But I really need it. I'm feeling guilty and I'm afraid if it goes on like this, I'll end up acting out or running away."

Gene was hurt at first, but eventually he understood and agreed to give Krista the time and space she needed. Krista discovered that being on the other end wasn't as bad as she imagined. Though it was uncomfortable for a while, she found that she enjoyed her time with Gene even more when she didn't see him every night. Having a few evenings a week to herself allowed her to spend time with her friends as well as to work on the art projects she'd been neglecting. Gene continued to press her for more of a commitment—but Krista found that contrary to everything she'd always believed, she was happy having a man in her life a few nights a week. For now, anyway.

Krista admitted to her Relationship Support Group one night a few weeks later as she stood in front of her easel: "It's actually a relief to realize I need time to myself. I feel like a burden has been lifted off me."

*Your mother never told you. . .*
*that your behavior with men says something*
*about what you need for yourself.*

## It Has Something to Do With You

Grasping for intimacy and experiencing rejection kept Sheryl feeling like a victim. When she realized that she also needed distance, it gave her back her power. Her realization is an example of what we call *owning your part*. Owning your part means recognizing that what happens in your relationships occurs because you are magnetizing it toward you or encouraging it to happen—whether knowingly or unknowingly. Owning your part is a powerful stance to take because it means that you have more to say about what is in your life. When you own your part you are recognizing that things don't just happen to you—they have something to do with you.

Owning your part means standing lovingly at the center of your life and taking responsibility for what is in it.

Being in charge of what's happening in your life doesn't mean blaming yourself or criticizing yourself. Owning your part means standing lovingly at the center of your life and taking responsibility for what is in it. There is no blame involved—just awareness. Owning your part can be a great relief because it allows you to know that if you don't like what is in your life, you have the power to change it.

To begin reflecting on owning your part, you can ask yourself, "Why is this here?" The answer will likely fall into one of the following categories:

*You are drawing toward you certain people and situations that you expect*
*You are living out beliefs that you developed early in life*
*You are having a hidden conversation that you haven't yet revealed to yourself*
*You aren't coming from a heartfelt place of loving yourself*
*You are making choices based on not being able to tolerate your feelings*
*You are repeating patterns from your past*

*You don't understand your power*
*You are acting on wrong information*

When you own your part you acknowledge that if something is happening in your life, it has *something* to do with you. This gives you the power to change it if you don't like it or reinforce it if you do like it. Krista saw that owning her need for time to herself gave her the power to have a good relationship with someone who wanted closeness. She could then take over the responsibility of measuring just how much distance she needed, and when. Instead of passively wondering what was wrong with her, she could be proactive in having what she wanted with a man.

When you live as if things were just happening to you, you give away your power. When you own your part, you are powerful because:

*You know that you have power in a relationship*
*You love yourself enough to set boundaries*
*You are awake and aware in the moment so you can make good decisions*
*You are working on your relationship with yourself*
*You take responsibility for selecting the man in your life*
*You are aware of your patterns*
*You have turned your back on what's not good for you*
*You don't blame him*
*You don't blame yourself*
*You accept that you are human and love yourself through the difficult parts*

When you own your part you begin to take charge. You are actively engaged in your life rather than just letting it happen to you—and you know you can attract the man and the relationship that you want.

When Sheryl identified her pattern of attracting men who were constantly pulling away from her, she owned her part in what kept happening. In that moment of recognition, she took back her power in relationship. She could keep herself from going into a conversation about what was wrong with her, why men didn't want to be close to her, and why no one could love her. Instead, she could have a man who cherished her and wanted to spend a lot of time with her—and she could be the one to say, "Could you move back a little? I need more room."

**When you own your part you begin to take charge.**

## Owning Your Need for Distance

Cynthia discovered that her need for distance originated in her mother's excessive need for closeness. It is possible that, like Cynthia, you had a parent who tended to get a little too close for comfort—either by getting under your skin as her mother did, or by being controlling, or by being a disciplinarian, or by having too much distance. It is sometimes difficult for parents to separate from their children, and it is natural for them to be involved in ways that may feel intrusive. To the degree that you felt uncomfortable with closeness or being controlled in childhood, you will need a level of distance in relationship. Yet it may be difficult to own your part in this, because as a woman you were brought up to believe that you wanted closeness and it was the man who wanted distance.

You were likely raised to believe that a man would be the center of your life, and you have probably been living out that belief to some extent—either consciously or unconsciously. Owning your need for distance may feel very uncomfortable because we were taught we should want to be close. You may already be someone who is good at maintaining a healthy distance, but most women are not.

To the extent that you think you will give up your independence and freedom for a man, there is a part of you that will be resentful, and that part will have things go sour in your relationship. Every woman needs a certain amount of independence and freedom, and only you know how much of that you need. It will be powerful for you to own your need for distance and to find a man who fits your needs.

> Every woman needs a certain amount of independence and freedom, and only you know how much of that you need.

By owning your need for distance, you will naturally feel surer of yourself. You won't always feel rejected when there is distance in the relationship that you, in fact, have chosen. When you say yes to a man even though you would really rather spend the evening by yourself or with your friends, you are not honoring a part of yourself. By contrast, when you own your need to have a night to yourself, take a weekend off from the relationship, and participate in activities that don't include him, you take your power back. He won't go away just because you are taking some time to yourself. And if he does go away, it wasn't meant to be.

## Being Willing to Be Wrong

It can be a difficult thing to admit we're wrong about something. We women in particular hate to admit we're wrong. In fact, we can get a little self-righteous at times when we think we have it all figured out. Yet when we own that we're wrong, we give ourselves the chance to change things for the better. If we're going to own that we attracted what we have in our lives, we need to be willing to be wrong about some things.

Sheryl had to be willing to be wrong about herself in order to have what she wanted. She had to admit that perhaps she wasn't the "Queen of Intimacy" after all, but that like everyone else she had a need for a certain amount of privacy and distance. It wasn't easy for her to be wrong about the identity she'd built for herself, yet she was willing to do it since it meant she could be happier.

Owning her part in her life and her relationships included being wrong about that central fact.

As women, we tend to be a little arrogant about men and think we understand them better than they understand themselves. Because we are better at arguing than most of them are, we can sometimes override their point of view. Yet it doesn't serve us to be strident. When we can lean back, breathe, and see that he might have a valid point, we allow him room to express himself. We are very good at expressing ourselves and can usually win an argument with him be-

Owning your part in what has gone wrong allows him to come forward and own his part too.

cause we can think well on our feet. Yet it's not always in our best interest to be right at all costs. Owning your part in what has gone wrong allows him to come forward and own his part too. And it gives you the power to say, "Here is the situation. What can we do to fix it?"

## Being Pleasable

How easy is it for a man to please you? Think about being opposite yourself for a moment and imagine trying to figure out how on earth to give you what you want. Women are very complicated and most men cannot fathom us. They really want to please us, but often they have no idea how to do it. And often we don't make it easy for them.

Krista learned an important lesson about being pleasable when she discovered how much Gene wanted to pay attention to her. She had always said she wanted a man to be devoted to her, yet once she had him she found herself wanting to rebuff his attention. When he wanted to look at travel brochures with her, she brushed him off, saying, "Oh, I'm far to busy to go away anytime soon."

Krista found that to get a grip on her behavior she had to sit herself down and own her part in having Gene in her life. "I asked for him, and he's here," she reminded herself. "And I need to remember that I'm responsible for him being here. I can be grateful for having what I asked for and be open to letting him please me."

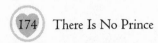

**We need to open our hearts and be willing to be pleasable.**

Believe it or not, men really want to make us happy—and a lot of the time we don't make it easy for them. We say we want something, but when it shows up we aren't satisfied. Because we've been raised with the expectation of finding a Prince, we are constantly holding our man up to the list of princely qualities he may not measure up to. How can a man please us when we are constantly comparing him to an unrealistic list?

It is important for us to own our part in not letting men give us what we want. We can be critical by nature and quick to judge. When we can own our critical nature it allows us to lean back a little and be easier with men. Instead of being so swift to criticize him when he doesn't please us, we can make sure to offer encouragement when he does. It is human nature to respond positively to encouragement and negatively to criticism. In order to encourage them, we need to open our hearts and be willing to be pleasable. When we are pleasable, it allows them to feel like heroes—and the more they feel like heroes the more they will give us what we want.

### Helping Yourself

When you don't own your part, you tend to act out in ways you may not understand. You might be cruel to the man in your life out of resentment—or you might turn your anger inward toward yourself. Either way, you end up sabotaging your chances for happiness. Ways you might do this include:

*Not being pleasable*
*Thinking there's something wrong with you*
*Being overly critical*
*Being overly possessive*
*Not admitting you're wrong when you're wrong*
*Nagging him*
*Starting arguments over something unrelated*
*Blaming him for not wanting you enough*
*Blaming yourself for not being lovable*
*Demanding a commitment*

Remember that you have attracted what is here and that if you don't like it, you can do something about it. It's easy to start feeling like a victim in your own life, and the cure is to lovingly acknowledge to yourself that you are in charge. When you notice yourself acting out in ways you don't understand, take yourself aside and examine whether you're really "owning" what you have in your life.

## When Cinderella Takes Matters Into Her Own Hands

In the film *Ever After*, Drew Barrymore plays a new version of Cinderella who takes matters into her own hands. When she is sold off to an evil lord and made to be his slave, she refuses to give in to him even though she's in chains. She tricks him into giving her the key to her handcuffs and frees herself. Rubbing her wrists, she leaves his dreary castle to find the Prince riding up to rescue her—too late! She has already rescued herself. Yet she is overjoyed to see him, and they are now free to have an equal, loving partnership.

You too can create your own modern-day fairy tale. Owning your part will have you free yourself of the bonds that have held you: your history, beliefs, hidden conversations, and patterns. You have the power to cast off what has been holding you back from having what you want with a man. And while you're concentrating on yourself and giving yourself what you need, you may be surprised to see that you are attracting men who will be good for you and who will give you what you want. They may start showing up just as the Prince showed up for the new Cinderella—not to save you, but to add to the quality of your life. When you own your part, you can have a fabulous relationship because you are taking responsibility for what you have.

*Your mother never told you...*
  *that if it's in your life, you have something to
  do with it.*


## But Women Don't Have Commitment Issues...

Once Sheryl owned her need for distance, she realized that she wasn't as ready for marriage as she'd thought. She saw that she needed more time before she would be ready to commit to Gene. She liked having her own apartment and didn't want to give up her private space. As a child, her mother hadn't allowed her to lock her bedroom door and would often barge in without knocking. As an adult, Sheryl was protective about her space and was reluctant to share it on a daily basis.

Owning her fear of commitment allowed Sheryl to be honest with herself and with Gene about what she was available to give to their relationship. Believe it or not, each and every one of us has commitment issues. It may be hard to admit that we have them when we've been taught that men are the ones who have trouble committing.

**We all have mixed feelings about commitment.**

Our culture supports the myth that men don't want commitment and women do. Like good girls, we follow that belief and push for commitment once we start getting attached to someone. Yet the fact is that we all have mixed feelings about commitment. You may not have realized that you have mixed feelings. If you were brought up to believe you would have a committed relationship with a man, you might not even have questioned whether or not you wanted one.

What you may not have realized is that if you're not in a committed relationship, you have commitment issues. Having commitment issues can look a lot of different ways. It can mean choosing men who won't commit, having every relationship end after three months, being dissatisfied with men because they fall short of being a Prince, not being able to decide if you want children, or leaving a relationship as soon as things aren't going well.

Even if you are in a committed relationship, you might have commitment issues. It's no wonder that over half of all marriages end in divorce. It is a very frightening thing to pledge yourself to someone for a lifetime. Committing to a man means having to consider him every day for the rest of your life. There he is—day in, day out, with his moods and his boxer shorts on the floor and his Sunday afternoon football game. When he's sick you'll have to take care of him, and when you want to move to a new house, buy a car, or go on a vacation you'll have to plan it with him. You'll share a bedroom, a kitchen, and perhaps a bathroom. All the habits and routines you get comfortable with when you're by yourself will be disrupted and you'll have to be flexible to accommodate his habits and routines.

**If you are not in a committed relationship, then there is part of you that doesn't want one.**

You'll have to compromise on some things and give in to him on others. You'll have to try to get along with his mother, his father, his siblings, and his friends—and perhaps even his children.

We women tend to hold onto our desire for commitment very tightly. And when we hold onto something so tightly, it's because we're afraid. If you're not sure you have issues with commitment, take a look at what is in your life right now. If you are not in a committed relationship, then there is part of you that doesn't want one. If all your committee members were in unanimous consent that they were ready for a commitment, you would be in a committed relationship. That's how it works.

*People have trouble committing*—not just male people, but female people too. You almost certainly have at least one committee member who doesn't want a commitment. She may be silent, and you haven't been aware of her until now. If you can't imagine you have a committee member who doesn't want to commit, just try on the idea for a while—because she's probably there somewhere, digging in her heels. She has good reason for not wanting a commitment. She is trying to protect you from being hurt, losing your personal space, or giving up your self for a relationship. In Sheryl's case, even her perception of herself was challenged when she started owning her part.

Your silent committee member's concerns are valid, and when you can turn up the volume and hear her hidden conversation, you may discover what's been holding you back from a commitment. She might be wary of commitment because:

*You've had your heart broken before*
*You had parents who were overbearing, critical, smothering, or too distant*
*You are already committed to your career*
*Your parents' marriage was difficult*
*You took a vow never to get married*
*You have given up your sense of self in relationship before and fear you'll do it again*
*Your parents really want you to get married and you are rebelling*
*You don't want to be like your mother*
*You enjoy being with a variety of men*
*You're afraid of being bored*
*You don't trust yourself to make the right choice*
*You're not sure you want to have children*

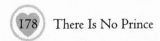

Women tend to be very fierce about wanting a commitment. Some of us put it forward quite soon in a relationship and we push for it constantly. We may not be doing it out loud, but we are sending out the signals clearly. And the more we send out "I want a commitment" signals, the more we push men the other direction. It's a simple law of nature. If one of us is leaning forward, the other has to lean back. And generally it's you that is leaning forward and he's the one that is leaning back, simply because of what you were brought up to believe and expect.

Even if you don't verbalize your need for a commitment, you're giving out messages that say, "Are you ready to commit? Why aren't you ready to commit? I want a commitment. When will you be ready to commit?" And he is saying, "No, no, no, no." This keeps you, like Sheryl, leaning forward and grasping for him while he has no choice but to lean back and pull away.

Finding the part of you that has mixed feelings will allow you to lean back a little more and express your ambivalence about commitment—and this will allow a man to lean forward a little more and own his desire to be with you. It's as if there are two opposite poles, one labeled "I need a commitment" and one labeled "No commitment." If you are holding on tightly to the "I need a commitment" pole, he has no choice but to hold onto the "No" pole. When Sheryl owned her need for distance, she was able to loosen her grip on the "I need a commitment" pole. She saw that commitment didn't have to come so soon and that she wasn't really ready anyway. And when she relaxed, it allowed Gene to come forward with his desire for commitment.

Owning her mixed feelings about commitment allowed Sheryl to have a new kind of conversation about it.

"You know, I have some mixed feelings about commitment," she said to Gene. "I want it, and I don't want it. It scares me because I don't want someone living under my skin like my mother did."

Recognizing your own ambivalence about commitment allows

you to lean back more and have a different conversation. Whether you have the conversation silently or out loud, he picks up on it—and when he knows you have doubts, he has room to lean toward you more. He might start thinking, "Oh no, she's not sure she wants a commitment. What if she doesn't want me?" He will have the space to get in touch with the part of him that does want a commitment. Rather than having to defend himself against your insistent need for commitment, he will be able to lean forward with his need for commitment.

**When you're more relaxed, you are more likely to attract what you want into your life.**

Getting in touch with the part of you that doesn't want a commitment can be an immense relief. You can let go of the pole you've been holding onto so tightly and relax a little more. And when you're more relaxed, you are more likely to attract what you want into your life. You are powerful when you are not worried about commitment, when you are owning your need for distance as well as your ambivalence about spending your whole life with him. You are powerful when you are leaning back a little more and expecting that he will come toward you.

*Your mother never told you. . .*
*that you'd have commitment issues, too.*

*Think about. . .*

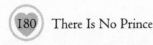 **Your need for distance.**
**Your mixed feelings about commitment.**

*The exercises for Chapter Eight can be found on page 268.*

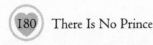

There Is No Prince

# CHAPTER NINE

# Understanding a Few Things About Men

Marilyn opened the second evening of the "Having What You Want With a Man" Workshop by saying, "We've been using up a lot of energy trying to figure out why the men in our lives aren't Princes. In other words, why aren't men fulfilling all our needs without being asked, treating us with unending patience and courtesy, giving us just the right gift, keeping all their promises, remembering all the important dates and anniversaries, and generally loving everything about us even when we're not behaving well."

A laugh of recognition traveled around the room. Marilyn continued, "We spend hours analyzing men with our girlfriends and hours agonizing about men when we can't sleep at night—don't we? Wouldn't it be great to understand men once and for all so we can stop expecting them to be different than how they are? We would start having great relationships with them. When we accept men for who they are and acknowledge that it's how they are supposed to be, we'll see how terrific they really are. We will be able to enjoy them—and they will be relieved.

"Remember the story of Oona the Martian who almost died because she'd been told water was green? We women are dying of thirst because we're looking for the green water. Yet there is plenty of good, clear, pure, thirst-quenching water right under our noses. But even when we decide to drink clear water, we think there's something wrong with it that it's not green. In other words, because we've been promised a Prince, we often end up disappointed when we find ourselves in relationships with real, live, walking, talking, human males.

"Why are we disappointed? Because they fall short of the princely ideal we've been promised. We all have lists of qualities we want our ideal man to have, don't we?"

Marilyn looked around to see that most of the women in the room were nodding. "Yes, we have lists, either written down or in our heads—and they're not short lists, either, right? We each have a list of a hundred and six qualities a man must have, and every man we meet gets compared to the lists. We hold up the lists and look at the men and they can't possibly measure up, so we're disappointed. We feel cheated. He's not a Prince!

"So we've become accustomed to living as though men will never live up to our expectations. If we want to stop being disappointed, we can change our expectations. Then we can change how we interact with men. We can open our hearts to them and accept them for who they are. We won't have to be critical and demanding. Men will respond positively to this because they want to be known and understood by us. It's good for us too, because when they are known and understood, men will give us anything we want."

> When they are known and understood, men will give us anything we want.

The room was silent, everyone's eyes riveted on Marilyn.

"So take out your notebooks and write this down. We need to start having different expectations, so here are some we can begin with. Why not live as though...

*Men are different from women*
*Men want to be treated well*

*Men want to be understood*
*Men are doing the best they can*
*Men want us to accept, appreciate, and understand them*
*Men are very attached to us and need us in their lives*
*Men want to be loyal, kind, and hear what we're saying*
*Men want us to be happy*
*Men want to give us what we want*
*Men need some help to know how to give us what we want"*

Marilyn waited for everyone to finish writing down the list.

"When we take a good look at how men really are and put away our lists of princely qualities they'll never measure up to, what are we left with?" she asked. "We're left with real people who want to love us, cherish us, and treat us well. There *are* a few men who don't want to do that. If you find one of those, don't go out with him. Most men really do want to make us happy—but we haven't been making it easy for them. I am going to help you understand some things about men that will allow you to be gentler, kinder, more patient, more compassionate, and more loving. And when you're that way, you will be loved the way you want to be. Men will be thrilled that you're seeing them for who they are and will want to give you the world."

> Most men really do want to make us happy—but we haven't been making it easy for them.

*Your mother never told you. . .*
  *that understanding men better will allow you*
  *to have better relationships.*

## Men Are Very Simple, Really

Marilyn stood up and surveyed the room. "Now I am going to tell you some things about men that might surprise you," she said. "Remember from the beginning of the Workshop when we talked about making me right? This is a good time to do that. Making me right means you will have to be willing to be wrong about some things. If you were right, you'd already have what you want with a man. So it's in your favor to have been wrong and to try on the new information I'm sharing with you. You may be tempted to start thinking of a lot of exceptions to what I'm about to say. And there are a lot of exceptions. I'm going to be talking in generalities. So it would serve you better to stay away from the 'except for sometimes' and make me right. Okay?"

Marilyn could feel the anticipation emanating from her audience. Most of the women were nodding, and some of them looked a little anxious. This was always an exciting moment in the Workshop.

"You may have noticed that compared to you, men are very simple," she began. "So this explanation is also going to be very simple. To really understand men, we are going to travel back to the time when we all lived in caves—because that's where it all started. Remember? We existed in caves longer than we've been out of them. And it was in the caves that the differences between men and women really began.

"So in the cave times, what did men do? They went out to get the meat. They protected the cave. That's what they did. Simple, right? Now, while they were out getting the meat and protecting the cave they did a lot of waiting—waiting for the animal to run past, or waiting for the enemy to come over the hill. So they had to think of a way to entertain themselves while they were waiting.

"One day a man reached down and scooped up some earth. He molded the earth into a sphere and then he threw it at his buddy. Instead of being hit with the sphere, his buddy held out his hand and caught it. And his buddy thought that was pretty neat, so he chucked the sphere back at the first man. They had such a good time that they did it again the next day, and the next. By the end of a week, the first man noticed his spear arm getting

There Is No Prince

stronger and realized this was a great way to get better at killing the meat and fighting the enemy.

"One day, another caveman took the branch off a tree, stripped off the twigs, and gestured to his friends to throw the sphere at him. When it came toward him, he swung the branch and hit the sphere with it. And the next day when they were doing it again, all the other clansmen wanted to join in, so they arranged a place for everyone to stand. And voila—a ball game!"

Marilyn laughed along with the Workshop participants. "So, what do men do? They go out and get the meat, they protect the cave, and they play ball. It's not complicated, is it? Then they come home. And what do they want when they get home? They want to be fed a hot meal. Not salad or cheese and crackers. They want a hot meal, and after the meal they want some physical affection. Then they want to be left alone. And then they want to go to sleep."

Marilyn paused, letting the information sink in.

"So this is what men do—let's start from the beginning. Say it along with me. The women, laughed, repeated: 'They go out and get the meat, they protect the cave, and they play ball. They come home and want to be fed, they want physical affection—then they want to be left alone, and sleep.'

"And that's it. That's men. And not a lot has changed since the cave times."

The room fell into silence again.

"And what do women do?" Marilyn went on. "*Everything else.* In the caves we bore and raised the children, planted, harvested, preserved, and cooked the food, dried herbs to use for healing illness, decorated the caves, tanned hides, and made sure there was enough clothing. We developed the ability to look back to the previous winter and remember that two of the elders froze to death because we didn't have enough fur. And when we remembered what happened last winter, we could look forward to the next winter and plan for it.

"Because we were in the caves with other women, we developed the ability to cooperate. We worked in circles and made sure everyone was included and taken care of. We made sure everyone was fed, happy, and comfortable. We became skilled comforters, communicators, cooperators, and empowerers. We planned together and talked things over together.

"We needed men and they needed us because all the jobs were crucial to survival. If the man didn't bring home enough furs, we'd get upset and make him go out and get more furs—so he would. It was a powerful exchange. This division of labor was around for so long that men's and women's brains developed differently.

"While they were out hunting for meat and protecting the cave, men developed the ability to strategize, to act quickly, to work within a hierarchy, and to be strong. They never knew which direction the meat would come from or when it would charge, or when the enemy would show up and how many men they'd have to fight. In order to get the meat or defeat the enemy they had to be able to be flexible, stay focused, think quickly on their feet, and take an action at the last minute. Survival of the fittest meant that the man who was quickest, strongest, and the best fighter would be the one to carry on the human race, so men's brains developed a keen ability to compete and to take quick action.

"Women, on the other hand, were programmed to plan ahead, remember the past, keep lists of details in our minds, and do many different things at once. We have pathways in our brains connecting the past to the future and it's easy for us to remember, plan, be detail-oriented, and multitask. Sometimes, of course, men can do these things—just as we can sometimes strategize and compete. Yet *expecting* men to do what we do will keep you disappointed. Their brains are different, and they are not like us. When we *expect* that they will be different, we can set up a healthier dynamic that will allow us more room for happiness.

"So." Marilyn took a deep breath. "That's the basics. That's where we need to begin in order to understand men. That's it in a nutshell."

She sat back down in her chair.

"As you continue to learn about men, I ask that you open your heart to them as much as you can. Some of us have been very defensive and angry with men—yet once we understand our own power and begin to understand them better, we can see that we don't need to be that way. When our hearts are open to ourselves, we know we can take care of ourselves so we don't have to walk around ready for a fight. We can know that men are not the enemy, and we can approach them with open hearts and appreciate what is wonderful about them. And when we appreciate them, they will appreciate us. Because women are the keepers of relationships, we are the ones who need to keep this heart-opening exchange going. It's a win-win situation."

> ❦
>
> **Men are not
> the enemy.**
>
> ❦

*Your mother never told you...*
*that men's and women's behavior was formed*
*in cave times and hasn't changed all that much*
*over time.*

## Men Don't Remember Like We Do

Women are really good at remembering details. We remember to feed the cat, take out the garbage, and pay the bills on time. We remember where the spare house key is hidden, what day yoga class is on, our friends' favorite foods, and what he was wearing the first time we saw him. And it often frustrates us when men don't remember details as well as we do. But his brain simply didn't develop the ability to remember details. He didn't *need* to remember back to last winter in the caves. Instead, he needed to be able to think quickly and take action in the moment. He needed to be able to smell an animal, identify its tracks, and know what it ate and when the herd would move to higher ground. He needed to think on his feet when he saw the enemy pounding down the hill toward the cave. He did not need to remember how it went last time, and in fact remembering how it went before could be an impediment to dealing with the immediate situation. So he didn't develop the ability to remember the way you did.

And therefore—men don't remember like you do.

Men don't remember—and we know this about them. We can't help but notice that they sometimes forget things like the fact that Monday is women's group night, that they got tickets to the game, and that next Thursday is Valentine's Day. They don't remember to wash the car and they forget to put their dirty clothes in the hamper. It slips their mind that the credit card bill is due in a week and that the family reunion is coming up at the end of the month. They don't remember to fix the toilet and they forget to clean the dead leaves out of the drainpipe. Of course they don't always forget *everything*, and some men are better at remembering than others. Yet no matter what their ability to remember, the fact is they forget a lot more than we do. And when we expect them to remember, we live in a state of anger and disappointment—partly because we take it personally that they forget.

> The only way to avoid the frustration, hurt, and blame that will ultimately damage your relationship is to understand and accept that he forgets.

Don't you usually take it personally when he forgets that he promised to research something on the computer or that your mother is coming for a visit? You think, "If he really loved me he'd remember." But in reality it has nothing to do with whether he loves you or not. It's a simple matter of biology. It's no accident that you're the one keeping track of the social calendar and the grocery list. You are programmed to be able to keep dates, lists, and priorities in your head—and he is not. It's that simple. When you take it personally it keeps you angry and disappointed, and he feels bad that he can't please you. He is insulted by your criticism because he didn't mean to harm you. And because he's insulted, he starts acting strangely and you don't know why. Yet the only way to avoid the frustration, hurt, and blame that will ultimately damage your relationship is to understand and accept that he forgets.

Once you've accepted that things slip his mind, you can do things to lovingly help him to remember—but he may never remember everything all on his own. You will feel better if you realize that he loves you *and* he forgets. And this can actually be a good thing. When you have that argument in the morning and you are stewing about it all day, there is something good in the fact that he has forgotten about it. He has not spent the whole day thinking of possible ways you are going to bother him when he gets home. If he had, he would be walking through the door ready to defend himself—perhaps offensively. Instead he walks in quite innocently every time because he has forgotten all about the argument or the fact that you are upset with him. Yet you have been thinking about it all day, so you hit him with it when he comes home and he is truly shocked.

You tend to think that because he hasn't thought about you all day it means he doesn't love you, right? But if you don't take it personally, it might actually benefit you that he can't remember everything. He doesn't worry every detail to death the way you probably do. Perhaps there is something you can learn from him about relaxing and not obsessively thinking things through.

Forgetting things doesn't bother him the way it bothers you. As a woman, you are an efficiency expert in many ways. Your brain is constantly categorizing what needs to get done, when to do it, and how long it will take. If you are taking your niece and nephew to the beach, you remember to bring Kool-Aid, sunscreen, and everything else you will need to make the day enjoyable. If you are giving a presentation at work, you remember to bring the notes you made last night. When you walk from the living room into the kitchen, you pick up the dirty glasses on the way, and if you forget to do it you are probably annoyed that you have to make an extra trip into the living room to get them.

Men are often not bothered if they have to make an extra trip. They are not efficiency machines. They are programmed to live much more in the moment and they are usually focused on what needs to get done right then.

At this point in the workshop, a woman in the last row raised her hand and offered her story. "Last week I was working at home, which is something I don't usually do, and my husband left for the office at 8 a.m. and then an hour later he was back because he forgot his appointment book. I felt a slight edge of annoyance and surprise that he would come all the way home for it. At 3:30 p.m. he was home again looking for notes for a class he had to teach that afternoon. I said, 'I can't believe you're back here again.' His response was, 'It's OK. It's a beautiful spring day and I enjoy being outside.' I could never have been OK with two trips home in one day. But it seemed OK to him!"

Expecting your man to forget allows you to take the charge out of it when he does. You can notice when he forgets and say with a smile, "Ah, there's my man forgetting. I have a real man on my hands," instead of thinking he doesn't love you because he didn't remember. And you can lovingly do things to help him remember. When you accept that he loves you *and* he forgets, you will be a lot happier and he will be relieved.

*Your mother never told you. . .*
    *that when you stop taking it personally when*
    *he forgets, you can have a calmer, happier, more*
    *loving relationship.*

## What "I'll Call You Tomorrow" Means to a Man

"I'll call you tomorrow," he promises after your date. But what does tomorrow mean? It might mean something different to him than it does to you. Remember the caves? Women have an excellent sense of past, future, and the passage of time. You possess an extraordinary ability to plan and to accomplish things over a long period. And because of the way his brain is programmed, he lives more in the present. The past and the future do not exist for him the way they do for you. He is great at acting spontaneously and making decisions in the moment, but it is impossible for him to keep a timeline in his mind the way you can.

> He is great at acting spontaneously and making decisions in the moment.

"We haven't been to see my sister in ages," you might say one Sunday afternoon.

"What! We were just there," he says.

"But we haven't visited her in over a month," you object.

"I'm sure we were just there last week," he insists. When you show him where you had it written on the calendar, he is truly surprised. You might have thought he was hedging to try to get out of visiting your sister—and then you would be offended and an argument could ensue. Accepting that his sense of timing is different from yours allows you to relax when he interprets it differently than you do.

You live between the past and the future, swinging back and forth from one to the other. And he lives in the moment without always checking to see what happened in the past to see what will happen in the future. This leaves him open to being inventive, to creating something new without worrying about what happened last time he tried it. He needs to get the job done in the moment and his mind is a clean slate because he is not remembering what happened in the past all the time like you are. His ability to be fresh in every situation is a wonderful quality if you can see it that way. He is a lot easier to please than

> He is a lot easier to please than you are.

you are. You remember the last time he tried something and how it didn't work, while he is concentrating in the moment on how to do it now.

A Workshop participant shared about watching her boyfriend and his friends make arrangements to go to the funeral of another friend's brother. "They agreed to meet at 1:30 p.m., which in my mind was not enough time to get there. When I mentioned it to my boyfriend, he annoyingly responded, 'It'll be fine.' When he got home he told me that they got there just after the service ended. Their friend, however, was not disappointed that they'd missed the funeral, but rather was touched that they'd made the effort and couldn't thank them enough for coming. Isn't that unbelievable?"

"That's just men being with men," said Marilyn. "Or rather how cavemen take care of each other."

A man's ability to be fresh in every situation can work to your advantage if you are not constantly fighting it. His perspective brings a clarity and lightheartedness to situations. You tend to get really serious and worried about things because you are programmed to look to the past and worry about the future. When you can lean back and see things his way sometimes, it can allow your relationship to be more enjoyable. Expecting that his sense of time will be different from yours can have you loosen your grip and relax a little. If he says he'll call you tomorrow, you think that means he'll call tomorrow. In fact, you think it means tomorrow morning. Yet it may be that tomorrow to him means ten o'clock tomorrow night, or even ten o'clock a.m. the day *after* tomorrow. Getting on his case about it will have him on the defensive because he is very sensitive to criticism. Understanding his sense of timing is another way to allow more ease into your relationship.

**When you can lean back and see things his way sometimes, it can allow your relationship to be more enjoyable.**

*Your mother never told you...*
  *that a man's sense of timing is different from yours.*

## Handling His Delicate Ego

Believe it or not, men are far more sensitive than we are. Their egos are extremely fragile, and the tough exterior they put on is designed to cover up the fact that they are very susceptible to being hurt—especially by the women they love. They saw the same movies you did and were subjected to the same cultural beliefs and expectations. They know they're supposed to be the Prince, and they also know they will never measure up to Antonio Banderas, Tom Cruise, Denzel Washington, Mel Gibson, Brad Pitt, Arnold Schwarzenegger, Clint Eastwood, or Joe DiMaggio. This leaves them susceptible to feeling humiliated and sensitive to the least criticism. They know you have a checklist of a Prince's qualities you are comparing them to, and they also know they can't possibly measure up—just as we can't measure up to a glamorous actress or an airbrushed *Playboy* centerfold.

Everyone hates criticism, but men have a particularly low tolerance for it—and we tend to criticize them a lot without realizing how much we're hurting them. The reason we don't realize we're hurting them is that they don't let us know directly. They don't say, "Honey, your critical remark about my dancing ability really hurt my feelings." Yet they *do* let us know they are hurt in a more indirect way. Knowing how to read the signs can help you understand when he is behaving strangely.

When a man's ego is bruised, he will do any or all of the following:

*Deny his feelings*
*Become emotionally distant*
*Go away*

*Break a promise*
*Begin an argument later about something seemingly unrelated*
*Withhold from you*

A man will not usually admit he is hurt. If you are afraid you've hurt him and you ask him if you've hurt him, he will probably say no. You can probably tell if you have, though, because he may be emotionally "gone" even though he's sitting right in front of you. Then he may actually leave for an hour, a day, or a week. You may not hear from him and you can't figure out why. He may respond to you by breaking a promise to call, meet you, or do something for you. Because he's hurt and he can't admit his ego is bruised, he may start an argument with you about something else later. When you wonder why on earth he's arguing with you so passionately about the phone bill, it's because it's too painful for him to tell you about what's *really* bothering him. And he probably doesn't even realize it himself. The next time you ask him to dance at a wedding and he refuses, he may be having a delayed response to being insulted.

He is probably not consciously doing any of these things, and if you confront him about it he is likely to deny it. His behavior is an unconscious defense because he is wounded. You probably won't get far if you try to talk with him about it, yet being aware of the reason he's acting the way he is can help your relationship.

Inwardly, you realize, "Ah, I must have offended him. I wonder what I said that hurt him. Oh yes, it must have been when I said he danced like he was churning butter and stomping grapes. Oops! Well, I'll let him go through what he needs to go through and I'll be extra gentle with him for a while. Then I'll expect him to be distant for a time. I'll apologize, and let him deny it bothered him—even though I'm sure it did. It would have bothered me if he said something like that to me. Once I've apologized, he will be able to relax and treat me better. And I'll remember not to joke about his dancing again."

Hurting a man's feelings in private is enough to wound him, but humiliating him in public can be devastating. *Men fear public humiliation more than almost anything in the world.* Of course, no one wants to be humiliated in front of others, but take your fear of public humiliation and multiply it by a hundred—that's how sensitive he is. He may appreciate that you're verbally quick and have a great sense of humor, but he won't appreciate it if it's at his expense. He may cover it up well, but he'll hold it against you. The more macho he acts, the more he is covering up his sensitivity. When you make a joke at his expense in front of his friends, put him down in front of the family, or do something that embarrasses him, it will take him a long time to get over it.

At this point in our workshop, a woman shot her hand up and exclaimed, "My last boyfriend and I used to go to street fairs. But we stopped because I noticed that after every one he picked a fight with me and made fun of me for bargaining. I wonder if I embarrassed or humiliated him by bargaining? In my family, being a good dealmaker was as asset. Wow, I guess I really didn't know how sensitive he was. Amazing!"

Men want to feel safe and know they'll be treated well. When a man does bad boy things—going away, breaking a promise, starting an argument, or withholding from you—it's because he doesn't feel safe. He knows he's vulnerable and he can't stand it. If he knows you'll treat his vulnerability delicately he *will* feel safe, however. When he knows he's safe you'll see how easy it is to love him. Be aware of his sensitivity, because you will be treated well and you will be more inclined to treat him well—and you will have a happier, more loving relationship.

> Men want to feel safe and know they'll be treated well.

*Your mother never told you...*
that a man is extremely sensitive and his ego is
wounded easily.

*Think about...*

Seeing the cavemen in the men around
you. Enjoy noticing how little has changed.

*The exercises for Chapter Nine can be found on page 269.*

# CHAPTER TEN

# He'll Be Your Hero If You Let Him

Men crave our positive attention. They want our praise, our compliments, and our acknowledgment. Yet we often let our critical nature take over. Men are very psychic and they hear our criticism, whether we voice it or not. And that can be the death of romance. We tend to blame men for not being tender enough, but actually they are very romantic. Believe it or not, it's *women* who often squelch romance because we are so critical of men's efforts. If they don't get it just right, we criticize them. And because they're so sensitive, if they feel they've gotten it wrong once they may not try again. Yet they truly want to make us happy and feel like heroes—if only we'd let them!

When a man is treated well and lavished with positive attention, he will do anything to make you happy. He knows that if you're happy, the relationship will go well and if you're unhappy, you'll both be miserable. How many times have you heard a man say, "I just want you to be happy"? You may not believe him because it doesn't seem like he's trying to make you happy. Yet he probably *is* try-

> When a man is treated well and lavished with positive attention, he will do anything to make you happy.

ing—it's just that he may not know how to do it. He wants to know how, though. In fact he is dying to please you—but he fails often for two reasons:

1. *He has no idea how to please you.*
2. *You are hard to please.*

Remember, the power to be pleased is in your hands. You must be pleasable. He wants to please you and he may have no idea how to do it. You are the expert on what makes you happy. If you're not sure what makes you happy, find out by paying attention to yourself. If you don't know, how on earth can he know? Men aren't born knowing how to make you happy, and they may not even know how to make themselves happy.

You may have been resisting helping him please you because you've been promised a Prince, and a Prince would know how to please you without your telling him. A Prince knows the right flowers to buy, the right music to listen to, the right restaurant to eat at, and the right gift to give. But since the man in front of you is a real human male and not a Prince, he needs your help. He wants to make you happy, yet his training in the caves didn't include the fine points of relationship. He knows this, and he is dying for you to tell him what you want—gently, with an open heart. When he asks you which restaurant you want to go to tonight, it's not an idle question. He wants you to tell him because he wants you to be happy. And when you are willing to help him lovingly, you will end up with exactly what you want.

> ℒ♥
>
> **He is dying for you to tell him what you want—gently, with an open heart.**
>
> ℒ♥

Gifts are an area of great confusion for a man. He wants to buy you a gift you will like, but he simply does not know what you want unless you tell him. It's a rare man who will be able to fathom exactly what you want, and most men are at a loss when confronted with gift buying. It's no accident that it's men who fill the stores at 5 p.m. on February 14$^{th}$ or 10 a.m. on December 24$^{th}$. They put it off because they are afraid they won't do it right. They can't read your mind.

How many times have you opened a gift from a man and had to swallow your disappointment at receiving something that is, in your estimation, totally inappropriate? He may either be trying to get you something he thinks you want—like that sequined sweatshirt you gave to Goodwill soon afterward—or something practical like the blender you've been saying you need for months. He'll think he did a wonderful thing and he will be confused and hurt by your disappointment.

"As you spoke about this, Marilyn, I got incredibly sad," a woman in the Workshop revealed. "A few weeks ago I asked my boyfriend to get a box off the top shelf of my closet. With the box came a dusty, but brand new pair of fuchsia leather gloves that had been a birthday gift from him two years ago. We both saw the tag still hanging from them. The pain in his eyes made me feel so selfish for never wearing them. If I had thought about how hurt and disappointed he'd feel when I didn't wear those gloves, I would have proudly worn them everyday until they fell off my hands."

The simple solution is to tell him exactly what you want. It may not be ideal to open a gift when you already know what it is—but at least you'll know it's something you want. He will feel like a success for giving you something you really like, and your whole relationship will be better.

Ways you can help him make you happy:

*Answer him when he asks you where you want to go or what you want to do*

*Compliment him when he does something that pleases you*

*Drop hints about what you like and don't like*

*Tell him when you consider something worth celebrating*

*Tell him a few things you'd like for your birthday, the holidays, or the anniversary of your first date*

*If he gets it wrong, be gentle, be grateful, and remember to help him get it right next time*

❧

**It's generous of you to help a man make you happy.**

❧

It's generous of you to help a man make you happy. It's generous both to yourself and to him, because it allows you to be happy and it allows him to feel like a hero. And when he's feeling like a hero he will be more inclined to make you happy. It's a circle of give and take that benefits both of you and strengthens your relationship.

*Your mother never told you...*
*that he would do anything to please you...if*
*he only knew what you wanted.*

## He Needs You to Lead the Way

A Prince knows what you want without you having to tell him—and he knows just how to manage a relationship with tact, timing, and charm. Yet a human male is usually not good at managing a relationship, no matter how much he wants to have one. In the cave times, he was mostly out hunting with the guys. He learned how to function quickly and efficiently in a male hierarchy, but he didn't have to learn how to manage the fine points of relationship. In fact, we were the ones managing relationships as we worked in community with the other women, children, and elders to ensure the survival of the clan.

Women are the keepers of relationship. It's a mystery that men ended up being the ones who are supposed to take the lead, because we're actually much better at it than they are. They weren't born with a special gene for knowing how to ask us out, when to suggest a weekend in the mountains, and how to know when it's time to get married. In fact *you* are the one who ought to be doing that! You need to be willing to be the one to gently nudge the relationship forward in a loving and timely manner.

**If you want pleasant surprises from him, pleasantly surprise him first.**

If you want pleasant surprises from him, pleasantly surprise him first. If you want a romantic evening, set one up. If you want an apology, apologize. If you want a compliment, give him one. If you want him to be generous, give to him with an open heart. A man is looking to you for guidance as you progress in your relationship because he *knows* he doesn't know how to do it. There will be things you need to do first—from a relaxed and openhearted place, without resentment. Being willing to go first without pressing or being strident about it will allow your relationship to grow and expand the way you want it to.

"You know, Marilyn, you're right about this one!" a Workshop participant said. "Whenever a big project at work ends, I look over at my husband and notice him for the first time in weeks. I see again how handsome he is and I am reminded why I married him. Then I realize that I've missed him while I was so preoccupied and plan a romantic evening for us. And he begins to lavish me with his romantic side again. He's always right there with me when I remember that I can start our romance again instead of waiting for him."

As the keeper of the relationship, you are creating the atmosphere for it to flourish. That is why it works for you to go first. Things you have to do first may include:

*Apologizing, or owning your part, when there's been an argument*
*Putting together a romantic evening*
*Complimenting him*
*Gently bringing up issues that need discussing*

*Sorting out how to work the finances in your relationship*
*Figuring out how he can help out around the house so you can have more time together*
*Planning vacations and keeping track of the social calendar*
*Buying gifts for family and friends*

Going first may seem strange to you because you were brought up to think that he ought to be the one to take the lead. After all, doesn't the Prince always go first and the Princess follows? It is natural to have a resistance to going first in relationship. Yet when you do go first, you will be a lot happier. You'll be able to set the pace and he will be relieved that you're doing it. He will probably follow your lead, and he will be more inclined to take the lead himself once he knows what you want.

*Your mother never told you. . .*
*that you were the keeper of relationship.*

### Get Your Head Out of His Belly Button

Because women are the keepers of relationship, men need us to be strong and centered in ourselves. We don't realize how much they count on us being strong, having our own lives, and loving ourselves. Being independent goes counter to our cultural wisdom that says a woman's life centers around a man. Everything in our upbringing conspires to tell us, either forthrightly or subtly, that we won't be happy unless we have a man at the center of our lives. At Life Works we call this "head-in-the-belly-button disease."

> **Men need us to be strong and centered in ourselves.**

On some level, we have all experienced living with our heads metaphorically buried in a man's belly button. When we are in a relationship we can lose our sense of ourselves and get involved with his every move. We can get so stuck in monitoring his psychological reactions that we forget our own, and then we spend a lot of energy asking ourselves questions like: Did he call? When is he going to call? Why didn't he call? Was I too eager? Was I not eager enough? Where is he now? Why isn't he at home? What is he thinking? What did he mean by that? How is he going to react? What should I do if he says "X"? What should I do if he says "Y"? Should I tell him? Should I wait?

"This is the thing I really need to work on, Marilyn," said Allaire. "It's probably what has ruined my last three relationships. Or maybe every relationship. When my mother got divorced, she never stopped talking about my father—scrutinizing his actions, thinking about him, and analyzing him—even though he moved across the country and married another woman! I realize the cure is a strong, loving relationship with myself. And I am going to do it. My being able to have a good relationship depends on it."

Men feel burdened by having our heads buried in their navels. Wouldn't you? Imagine how you'd feel if he had his head buried in *your* belly button. They can't stand such an intense focus. They didn't sign up for the job of making us happy, and it puts them off when their every word and move affects our mood for the day. They want us to have our own lives, know who we are, and not be obsessed with them. This doesn't come naturally to us because we were raised to believe relationships were central to our existence. Yet when we can have a loving relationship with ourselves and get our heads out of their navels, we'll all be happier.

**They want us to have our own lives, know who we are, and not be obsessed with them.**

*Your mother never told you...*
   *that he wants you to be strong, happy, and have your own life.*

## Don't Pressure Him

Men react negatively to pressure and confrontation. Picture yourself standing with your hands on your hips, tapping your foot. A man doesn't want you to be his mother, telling him what to do and when to do it. He responds better to a gentle, understanding approach—just as you do. Because men's egos are delicate, they interpret your pressure as his inability to meet your demands. And when a man feels pressured, he retreats.

Things that make him run away include:

*Pushing him faster than he can go*
*Telling him he is doing it wrong*
*Breathing down his neck*
*Being his victim*
*Being bossy*
*Not thinking enough of yourself*
*Being disappointed*
*Watching for him to be wrong*
*Never being grateful*
*Not being pleasable*

Women tend to get demanding rather quickly in relationships because we are constantly looking toward the future. We can see what we want down the road and we sometimes forget that it will take time to get there. And because we are afraid we won't get what we want, we can be strident. We don't realize that if we could lean back, it will come to us when it's time. It's important to remember that we have the power to magnetize what we want toward us.

While you are worried about the future or stewing about the past, he is living in the moment and probably enjoying the relationship the way it is. When you hit him with pressure or demands, he has to retreat because you're coming on so strong. Usually when you're coming on strongly it's because you're feeling bad. You may be afraid things won't work out, impatient for things to move forward, or feeling out of control. When you can't tolerate your feelings you want him to make you feel better. Instead of making demands on him, you can share your softer feelings and let him comfort you. When you can relax a little, tolerate your feelings, and be patient, he will have room to come forward.

*Your mother never told you. . .*
*that when you pressure him, he is likely to*
*retreat.*

## They Really Can't Live Without Us

Men can't stand it when we're not strong. When we are sick or debilitated in any way they feel help-less. Have you noticed how difficult things are for a man when you are ill or out of commission in some way? He can't stand it. And the reason he can't stand it is that he's afraid of losing you. He gets very attached to you.

**When you can relax a little, tolerate your feelings, and be patient, he will have room to come forward.**

Deep down, men feel they cannot live without us. They are afraid we'll leave them and they don't know what they'll do. You may have noticed that when men are widowed or divorced they will often marry again very soon, while women tend to spend longer periods alone. This isn't necessarily because it's easier for men to find women, but because they can't stand being alone. Yet they do a lot of strange things to cover up this vulnerability.

Often men's macho or "bad boy" behavior stems from a deep knowledge of their attachment to us and their fear that we'll leave. They can't stand feeling vulnerable so they act badly to cover up their fear. If they knew fear was what they were feeling, they would be very humiliated—so they do things to push us away. Yet their behavior may often be in direct opposition to what they are feeling.

We think we're more attached to them because we're accustomed to making them the center of our lives, and they don't make us the center of their lives in the same way because they have been brought up differently. Yet even though it may not look like we're at the center of their world, men get far more attached to us than we are to them. It's a quiet, unconditional, unconscious attachment, and it is powerful.

A woman in the workshop shared, "What you are saying is so true. My last boyfriend always got sicker than me whenever I got sick. And when I was traveling for business he always sounded so sad when he answered the telephone. Like his light was dimmed when I was away. It used to make me angry. Now I see that he might have been frightened when I was sick, and lonely when I was out of town. He would never have admitted it. But now I can see it as an expression of his love and attachment to our relationship."

> Knowing how attached he is to you can help you be confident enough to live your own life while you are in a relationship.

Knowing how attached he is to you can help you be confident enough to live your own life while you are in a relationship. He probably won't leave because you take a night off to go out with your friends—and if he does, you are well rid of him. In fact, he will probably be relieved that you are taking some time for yourself. He knows that when you're taking care of your needs you will be more pleasant and gentle with him. You will be more available to be loving and less likely to criticize him because you are strong and centered in yourself. And he wants you that way.

*You*r mother never told you...
   *that he may be more attached to you than you*
   *are to him.*

## They're Not Fairy-Tale Princes...

It's strange that although we focus on men, sometimes to the point of obsession, we often don't see them as three-dimensional human beings. We all have mental lists of princely qualities they ought to have. We're often so busy comparing them to the lists that we miss the fullness of them. In fact, we can tend to see them as an accessory to our lives. We ask ourselves questions like: "Does he pay enough attention to me? Does he think of me often enough? Does he dress well enough to be seen with me? Does he make enough money? Is he good-looking enough? Does he fulfill my image of the Prince?"

Because we are taught that our self-worth is tied to having a man, we look at them through a filter of our own needs and desires. We don't always see that a man is a separate being with his own interests, preferences, opinions, and needs. We just want to hold him up against a list of princely qualities and check off the ones he has. And if he has enough of them, we decide he's the one. Yet we may not even really know him for who he is.

Knowing who he really is means knowing how he feels about his family, the style of life that makes him happy, his insecurities on the job, how important his friends are, that he loves Chinese food, that he hates having his hair cut, and that

> **Men want us to know and understand them.**

he doesn't want to talk in the morning until he's had a cup of coffee. It means replacing the list of princely qualities with a personal, meaningful, realistic list. Men want us to know and understand them. They respond well when we know them for who they are rather than comparing them to an ideal that they can never live up to.

The unrealistic lists come out when we are upset—and they probably don't have much to do with him. When you start comparing him to a list you can see it as a wake-up call, a signal that tells you you're already in trouble. Instead of making him the problem you can say to yourself, "I must be in trouble. Something else is going on with me. What is really wrong? How can I help myself?" Maybe the real problem is that you are afraid of getting too close, that you are feeling badly about yourself, or even just that you are about to get your period.

> **We need to provide a heartfelt, open, and accepting environment so men can give us what we want.**

When you can relax into yourself enough to get your head out of his belly button, you can start understanding what it is like for him to be opposite you. You can start really seeing him as a separate entity, not as someone who does or does not fulfill the qualities you think a man should possess. And this is a relief for him. He wants you to know him, and when he feels known he is available to respond positively to you and give you what you want.

*Your mother never told you...*
   *that it is essential to know and understand him.*

### ...But Plenty of Them Will Act Princely

Men want nothing better than to give us what we want. But we've thrown a lot of obstacles in their way. We've been too busy blaming men for not being Princes to let them make us happy. But once we understand who they are, we can let them make us happy. Because men are simpler than we are, they just have three requirements in order to be able to give us everything we want.

*1. They need to be treated well*

*2. They need to be known and understood*

*3. We need to make it easy for them*

In other words, we need to provide a heartfelt, open, and accepting environment so men can give us what we want. Once you understand who men are and why they behave the way they do, you'll also have to be willing to do what works. That doesn't mean you are giving in to him. It means providing a setting that will allow you both to be happy and have what you want. And having what you want with a man requires:

*Realizing he is not a Prince*

*Understanding who he really is*

*Understanding why he is that way*

*Realizing that most men are that way*

*Being willing to do what works*

You are the one with the power to have a great relationship. Men are dying to be close to you, be loved by you, and give you what you want. Once you are willing and available to work with them instead of against them, men will be greatly relieved and will do and say things you may never have dreamed were possible. Although there is no Prince, when you relax, understand him, and love him from your heart, he will become "princely" in your eyes—and you will be surprised at how often you'll feel like a princess.

**You are the one with the power to have a great relationship.**

*Your mother never told you. . .*
*that when treated well, most men would be*
*"princely."*

*Think about…*

 Observing men who want to make women happy. Watch for it in your daily life

*The exercises for Chapter Ten can be found on page 270.*

# CHAPTER
## ELEVEN

# *Knowing Your Power*

When we "own our part" in what happens in our lives—that is, when we see our own motivations, desires, and responsibility for what we have—we take back our power. We've been giving it away for a long time by not admitting to ourselves that we have something to do with what we have. In our era, we no longer have to be like Cinderella, Snow White, or Sleeping Beauty—we don't need to wait for the Prince to make it all happen. We're the ones who have the power to attract the relationship we want. Men want relationships with us. They don't want to live without us. A recent study showed that married men actually live longer than single men. Men know they want what we have to offer—but they don't know how to manage a relationship. They are built for action and spontaneity, and not for having the foresight, creativity, patience, ability to nurture, and communication skills it takes to cultivate a healthy, lasting bond. We are the ones who know how to nurture and cultivate a good relationship because we naturally have the abilities it takes.

As a woman, you have available to you the perfect combination of strength and softness to have a good relationship. Your female nature is wonderfully suited to cultivating relationship. In fact, as a woman you are the keeper of relationship. You are the one who has the power to communicate, to nurture yourself and him, to be tender, compassionate, and to know intuitively how to make the relationship satisfying for both of you. You are the one who knows how to keep a relationship sensual, rich, and satisfying. Being a woman means you possess all the qualities necessary for a relationship to be not only good, but also divine.

> *Being a woman means you possess all the qualities necessary for a relationship to be not only good, but also divine.*

## Attributes of Female Power

You are attuned to relationship in a way that men are not. Men know this and they are looking for you to be the leader. A good relationship needs the qualities that come naturally to you when you are loving yourself. When you are having a good relationship with yourself, you have all the power you need to attract the man you want and have the relationship you want. When you are centered and strong, you have the following qualities to share—qualities that are essential in relationship.

### We Are Natural Nurturers

Women are natural nurturers. We have an innate ability to know when someone needs care and how to give it to them. Just as we know how to soothe a baby to help stop her crying or help a friend who is in distress, we know how to nurture a relationship. We have a sense of pacing and balance that can have a relationship grow and flourish under our care. And the most important relationship we need to nurture is our relationship with ourselves. When we are tending our own garden, we will attract healthy men into our lives.

> *Our ability to nurture means we can put ourselves in someone else's shoes and know what it is like to be them.*

Our ability to nurture means we can put ourselves in someone else's shoes and know what it is like to be them. Understanding how men are can give us a strong sense of compassion for them. Instead of being fierce about what we need or what we think is right, we can pause for a moment and see how it looks to him.

## We Have a Strong Sense of Cooperation

When women were living in the caves, we had to learn to co-operate with other women to raise children, grow crops, prepare food, make clothing, and care for the sick. We still have a strong sense of co-operation. When we realize we don't need to be in competition with each other or with men, we naturally work to-gether to get things done and solve problems. We can use this skill in rela-tionship to work with him on the problems that come up. Coop-eration allows us to find win-win solutions. When we don't have to hold on fiercely to what we think is right, we can lean back a little and work together to make a relationship wonderful.

Cooperation allows us to find win-win solutions.

## We Are Effective Communicators

We are generally more verbal than men and we are accus-tomed to getting our point across effectively. Men can be daunted by our ability to argue and verbalize, and sometimes we use it against them. A large part of relationship is being able to listen. When we are willing to sit back and lis-ten to him with our hearts open, he will be able to tell us what he wants us to know—what he dreams of and what he wants to share. We can improve the qual-ity of communication in a relationship. Men get frustrated when they can't get their point across to us or when we override them. When we are willing to be wrong, not take things personally, and really listen, we will hear more from men.

A large part of relationship is being able to listen.

## We Are Naturally Tender

Tenderness is an expression of love. Because our bodies are designed for having and nurturing children, we naturally have a large capacity for tenderness. Yet we've gotten away from being gentle because it can be seen as weak. We often push to have our needs met rather than allowing ourselves to be tender. When we know we will be getting a real man and not a Prince, we can relax into our natural ability to be gentle, caring, and soft. Being gentle and acting from an open heart will allow him to feel safe enough to be able to express his own tenderness.

> Being gentle and acting from an open heart will allow him to feel safe enough to be able to express his own tenderness.

## We Are Healers

Women are natural healers. We know how to kiss a "boo-boo" and make it better, help a friend through a crisis, and show compassion when a man suffers a setback. When we're in a relationship, we need to be open to our healing power so we can help ourselves heal our past. When we're living from past hurts and past grudges, we can't be open and available to what is here for us now. We need to be our own healers, present and loving for ourselves as we create the relationship we want.

## We Empower Ourselves and Others

Empowering ourselves means believing in ourselves and allowing ourselves to be the healthiest and happiest we can be. Empowering a man means believing in him and allowing him to express himself fully so he can be the best person he can be. And empowering a relationship means giving it room to grow, believing it can work, and trusting that it can be everything both of you want it to be.

## We Can Know

"Women's intuition" is not a myth. Sometimes we just know what we know, and we don't know why we know it. We can use this sixth sense to help lead and guide us as we seek and experience relationship. When we are relaxed and our hearts are open, we are available to access our natural powers of intuition. Intuition can help us know when a man is good for us or when we need to get out of a situation. Often our thoughts and fears get in the way of our intuition, yet when we trust ourselves we will be able to allow ourselves to be guided by it.

> We have the power to design a relationship that will fit what we want.

## We Are Creators

Just as our bodies physically possess the ability to create new life, we also possess unlimited powers of creativity.

When we use our creativity in conjunction with our intuition, we have the power to design a relationship that will fit what we want. We can come up with imaginative solutions for problems and ingenious ways of being with someone that will suit our needs and desires.

## We Have the Power to Envision and Manifest

We can use our intuition and our creativity to envision the man we want to be in a relationship with. Then we can attract him to us. We have the power to create an image of what we want and magnetize it into our lives. The more clearly we imagine it, the more likely it is we'll have it. When we are tuned into our power of envisioning, it can be an incredible way to have what we want materialize.

> We have the power to create an image of what we want and magnetize it into our lives.

## We Are Naturally Open

When we are open, it means that our hearts are free to love ourselves and him, our minds are open to hearing his point of view, and our arms are spread wide to embrace what comes toward us. It means we are present in the moment and not repeating patterns from our history. It means we are available to accept him and also to accept our own humanity. To the extent that we are closed off, we won't be able to attract the man and the relationship we want. To the extent that we are open, we invite in the experience of love and satisfaction.

## We Are Naturally Receptive

When our hearts are open, we can take in the love that is all around us. When we're closed off, we push love away, and we may not even recognize it when it's coming toward us. Some of us have become very defensive about receiving because we're afraid of being hurt. When we have our hearts open to ourselves we don't need to be afraid. We can be free to enjoy the love and attention we want and deserve. On the other hand, when we are being fierce because we are unsure of ourselves, when our hearts are not open to ourselves, when we are repeating patterns from our past, and when we are not owning our part, it is difficult to be in the flow of our receiving, female nature. And this is most often when we will have difficulty in relationship.

A juicy, satisfying relationship needs your tenderness, your empathy, and your willingness to be vulnerable.

A juicy, satisfying relationship needs your tenderness, your empathy, and your willingness to be vulnerable. It needs your nurturing, your ability to communicate and cooperate, and your intuition. When you are in touch with your female nature you know instinctively how to help someone feel better, when to listen and when to give advice, what someone needs even if he doesn't know what he needs, and how to lean back and let things happen instead of using force.

*Your mother never told you. . .*
   *that a man would be lucky to be with a multifaceted woman like you.*

## Remember How Powerful You Are

Because you are the keeper of relationship, when you are happy your relationship is probably going well—and when you are unhappy, your relationship may be in trouble. Men are very psychic and they know when something is wrong, even if you aren't telling them out loud. When you're unhappy, disappointed, dissatisfied, or angry, a man will pick up on your feelings. He'll respond, perhaps unconsciously, to your mood.

When you don't understand your power in your relationship, you may be holding things against him or holding things against yourself. Perhaps without realizing it you are constantly conveying to him your emotional state. And he knows something is bothering you—but he probably doesn't know what to do about it. He may end up feeling helpless, victimized, and frustrated, which may lead him to act out by picking fights with you or disappearing for a while.

A man also listens to the tone of your voice when you talk to him. In fact, he may listen more to your tone of voice than to what you are saying. He is very sensitive to your tone and will probably respond in kind. If you're not feeling powerful, you may speak to him more

*A man also listens to the tone of your voice when you talk to him.*

forcefully than is necessary. When you can relax into the knowledge of your own power, you won't need to speak to him stridently. You will know that you can take care of yourself and have what you want, so you won't need to be forceful about it. This will make your relationship a lot easier and more pleasant.

Another way to keep your relationship satisfying is to give him back the problem he gives you. Instead of immediately reacting to a problem he presents, you can take a few breaths and remember how powerful you are. You can remind yourself that you don't have to feel threatened just because he is having a problem. You don't have to take on responsibility for what is his. Just as you own your part, you can help him own his part by handing him back the problem he's giving you.

> Having a satisfying relationship starts with you.

Having a satisfying relationship starts with you. Remembering how powerful you are will allow you to relax into your female nature, love yourself, and own your part.

Remembering your power means:

*You can know how powerful you are and not have to be demanding about it*

*You can trust yourself to take care of yourself*

*You can understand him for who he is*

*You can lean back a little more so he has room to lean toward you a little more*

*You can release your grip on the "commitment" pole and start nurturing your relationship with yourself instead*

*You can turn toward what is good for you instead of holding onto a pattern you've been repeating*

*You can know you have the power to attract whatever it is you want*

*You can stand strongly in the center of your life, knowing that what you have is here because you have created it*

*Your mother never told you...*
    *that you are very powerful in relationship.*


*Think about...*

 **Notice yourself being powerful in a female way.**


*The exercises for Chapter Eleven can be found on page 271.*

# CHAPTER
## TWELVE

# The Man You Want
# Is Out There

Wouldn't it be nice to be able to choose what
you want with a man and get it, like ordering food in a restaurant?
"I'll take one caring man, athletic, who has a good relationship
with his mother and wants to cherish me. And can I have a side
of a large bank account, please, and I'll finish with a beautiful
house. Oh, what do I want to drink? How about a pint of likes
to travel. Thanks—and oh, I'm kind of in a hurry so can you ask
the chef to put in my order ASAP?" Of course you can't just
choose a man from a menu, yet you do have a lot more choice
than you may realize.

You make choices every day about what clothes to wear, what
music to listen to, what kind of job to have, where to go for dinner, which movie to see, and when to go to bed. Yet you probably
don't approach having a relationship with a man the same way.
You may not realize that you have the power of choice when it
comes to having what you want with a man—and there is a reason you don't realize it.

Historically it was the man who did the choosing, and the
woman's role was to either accept or reject his overtures. Men and
women's roles have shifted drastically in the past forty years, yet
many of the old expectations remain. Because you are conditioned

to think that men are the ones who can choose, on some level you've been waiting for the Prince to arrive on his horse and choose you—without realizing that you can be the one to choose. You have the same level of choice when it comes to relationship as you do when it comes to picking a job, a car, or a place to live.

What is in your life is here because you have chosen it.

It is important to understand that what is in your life is here because you

have chosen it. You are making choices all the time, either actively or passively. If you never go out with a man for more than two months, you have made a choice on some level to end relationships before they get too serious. You may have made that choice without realizing it because it is based on your history, your expectations, your beliefs, and hidden conversations. You may not have known why you made the choices you made simply because you weren't aware of your hidden motivations. Becoming aware that you are constantly making choices gives you your power back. In fact, you have the power to choose what you want in a man— and have him come to you.

*Your mother never told you...
that you had the power to
choose the man and the relationship you want.*

You won't find a Prince, but you will find a real man who can act princely when he's treated well, understood, loved, and appreciated.

Like the thousands of women who created the relationships they wanted after taking the Workshop, you can give yourself the gift of having the relationship you want. We have developed a system of making lists and interviewing that helps you attract the man you want and the relationship that fits you. You won't find a Prince, but you will find a real man who can act princely when he's treated well, understood, loved, and appreciated. Women who have used our system often find the results stunning. They discover that they have the power to find just what they want—while loving themselves, nurturing their relationship with themselves, and being easy with themselves.

The man you want is out there. He's been waiting for you to love yourself, open your heart to him, and shift your old patterns and expectations so you can finally see him. He may be the one you've been overlooking in the elevator every day, the one you dated for a while and turned into your friend, or he may be coming around the corner any minute. And if the one coming around the corner isn't him—there's always another one coming. Men want relationships with women, and there is a man who wants a relationship like the one you want with a woman just like you.

There is likely a part of you that has a hard time believing that there is a man who wants to open his heart to you, cherish you, and build a satisfying relationship with you. Like many of us, you have probably had experiences of settling for someone who isn't good for you or right for you because you were afraid it might be your last chance. It's scary to turn your back on what's not good for you, but when you do you will be pleasantly surprised to find how much love there is all around you. You know that you deserve to have the relationship you want, and you deserve to be happy—and you can be.

You aren't designed to go through heartbreak after heartbreak. It used to be that a woman would marry in her teens or early twenties and stay with her husband until she died. Maybe she would have one love affair with a high school sweetheart before she got married—but she didn't have numerous relationships and get her heart broken over and over again.

Today we are dating for decades, having relationships without

*There is a man who wants a relationship like the one you want with a woman just like you.*

getting married, and going through divorces. And each time a relationship ends it is painful, it closes us off, it saps our energy and leaves us exhausted. It's no wonder we are wary and weary. Yet you can have what you want without having to go through a series of heartbreaks.

Snow White, Cinderella, and Sleeping Beauty were all powerless to do anything but wait for Prince Charming to show up on their doorsteps. And to some extent we have all been doing the same thing. We have been thinking that relationship is just something that happens to us rather than something we can choose carefully for ourselves. We have

*You can have what you want without having to go through a series of heartbreaks.*

tended to fall into the arms of a man whom we find attractive, or grasp onto whatever man pays attention to us, without taking the time to find out if he will be good for us or right for us.

If you have ever...
*Settled for someone because you didn't want to be lonely*
*Fallen in love with someone who wasn't good for you*
*Tried to change someone so he would be what you want*
*Stayed in a bad relationship*
*Been with someone who didn't want what you wanted*
*Ignored the signs that it wouldn't work*
*Said "yes" when you meant "no"*
*Didn't take care of yourself in the relationship*
... then you know how painful it is to be in the wrong situation with the wrong man.

You no longer need to just roll the dice and hope they turn up a winner. When you are lovingly engaged in creating your own life, you can magnetize toward you the man and the relationship you want.

*Your mother never told you...*
that you could choose the man you want.

## Conscious Choosing

Meeting the man you want can happen at any time. Many women who take our Workshops report that it can happen eas-

> *Meeting the man you want can happen at any time.*

ily—after they've become more open, awake, aware, and loving. Like them, rather than waiting for someone to come along and hoping he'll be the one, you can know clearly what you want and find out quickly if he should be considered.

If not, you can spare yourself a lot of heartbreak by not seeing him again. Beverly's grandmother always told her, "Men are like streetcars—there's always another one coming." When she started meeting men daily, she learned to simply say, "Next!" if he didn't fit what she wanted. We call the process *conscious choosing*. When you are choosing consciously you can magnetize toward you what you want. Conscious choosing means:

*Loving yourself*

*Actively working on your relationship with yourself*

*Not taking things personally*

*Being aware of your patterns*

*Owning your part in what happens*

*Understanding how men are*

*Being willing to experiment with men who look different from the ones you've always been with*

*Being clear about what you are looking for in relationship*

*Actively seeking out opportunities to meet men*

*Interviewing men to see if they match what you want*

*Saying "no" when he's not right for you*

*Moving slowly until you're sure he's right for you*
*Knowing that if he's not right for you, there's another one around the corner*
*Being awake and aware in the moment*

To engage in conscious choosing, you must first be willing to get off the couch and go out with someone new. This may feel uncomfortable if you haven't been out with a man in a while or if you've always jumped right into a re-

> ✍
> **Men are like street-cars—there's always another one coming.**
> ✍

lationship. Yet it is necessary to be willing to meet new men if you are going to find someone you want to be with. As you meet men you can think of it as an adventure, a process of sampling what is available that is a powerful way to discover who you are and what will make you happy.

## Your mother never told you. . .
### how to choose consciously.

## Making Some Lists

We are going to help you make lists that will help you have what you want with a man. You may already have a mental or writ-ten list of the qualities your man must have. Yet your list has not helped you have the man you want. The new lists you create will come from an openhearted place of loving yourself. They will speak to what you want today as a self-loving woman who is ready for a good man to come into her life.

If you haven't already made the list called "What I Want a Man For," you will want to make it now. As you go about making the rest of your lists, you will want to set aside some time for your-self. Your lists will help you the most when they come from a deep, loving place within you—not from outside circumstances in your life. If you are seeing someone, you may be tempted to make the list fit his qualities. But for the list to work for you, it's crucial to make it without reference to any man who is in your life right now.

The lists are for you, based on what you've learned about yourself, your patterns, and what you want. Your lists will be an invaluable reference to help keep you centered and connected to what you want while you are meeting men. You'll want to keep them handy and available to check if each man you meet fulfills your needs. And no matter how appealing he may be, the lists will keep you aware of what is good for you and able to turn away from what's not good for you.

> Your lists will be an invaluable reference to help keep you centered and connected to what you want while you are meeting men.

### List #1: The Six "Musts"

The six "musts" are the attributes a man absolutely must have for you to consider him—and if he doesn't have these qualities, you will eventually break up with him because of it. If you "must" have a man of your own religion and he is not, you will eventually break up with him because of it—right? If he "must" want to get married and he doesn't want to marry you, that will also be something that will eventually cause you to end it. If you want to have children, then he must want to have children.

How many women have you seen suffering because their man doesn't want to get married and they do, or their man doesn't want to have children and they do? If you want to get married and have children, put those as two of your "musts." If you want someone to share your religion, that would be a third "must." If you want someone with a certain amount of financial stability, that's a fourth "must." The rest of your "musts" might have to do with where he lives, how much time he can spend with you, his moral code, whether or not he has children by a former wife, or anything that is of supreme importance to you.

A "must" is a deal breaker—and you know what they are. If you wouldn't break up with him because of it, it is *not* a "must." The "musts" are the key as you begin the process of meeting, attracting, and interviewing men. They are designed to save you time, trouble, and heartbreak.

How many more heartbreaks can you stand? You have already had more than your share, and now you can be gentle with your heart by not getting involved with someone you'll end up breaking up with. You can allow your heart to be open to yourself through the process of conscious choosing rather than closing it off because you're afraid of getting hurt. You will know that if a man doesn't have your six "musts," chances are very good that it won't work out. Instead of having a six-month or two-year relationship before you discover it won't work, you can know on the first date or two—before you get really attached to him and your heart gets hurt again.

Knowing your "musts" will keep you out of the trap of thinking "It doesn't matter," "He'll change," or "He'll be different with me." Once you ascertain that a man doesn't have your six "musts," you will be able to gently say "no" to another meeting. It can be difficult to say no, yet when your heart is open you will find the strength to say it because you will know you are taking care of yourself. You will love yourself enough to refrain from seeing him again even if you find him attractive. Instead you can remind yourself, "Men are like streetcars—there's always another one coming!" You can make room for the next one to come along by saying to yourself, "Next!"

How do you find out on a first, second, or third date if he wants to get married and have children or what his attitude about money is? It may work to ask him straightforwardly, but there are more subtle ways of finding out, too. You can relate a story about a friend getting married or having a baby and see how he reacts, or you could go to a movie that focuses on marriage and family and talk about it with him afterward. If he is enthusiastic about family, you might consider another date with him. But if he says strongly that he doesn't want to get married or have children, you would not go out with him again. "Next!"

Your "musts" come from a heartfelt place of knowing and trusting yourself. It's important to list six of them—no more and no less. Six is a reasonable number that a man could live up to, and it also means you're not being overly picky or not discerning enough. A woman who is too choosy is probably afraid, and a woman who is not being careful enough is not loving herself enough. Now would be a good time to get rid of that list of a hundred and six "musts" you have in your bedside drawer. A real man could meet six "musts," but not a hundred and six.

Once you've come up with your six "musts" from a heartfelt place of caring about yourself, you will want to keep them intact. If you go out with a really appealing man who only has three of your "musts," you may be tempted to change them. But before you say blithely, "Oh, I didn't really want to have children," and cross it off your list—remember that you will eventually break up over this. To spare yourself the heartache you will inevitably go through later if you change your list, remind yourself to steer clear of the man who doesn't have all the "musts"—no matter how attractive you find him.

*It is an act of self-love to refuse to see someone again who will eventually break your heart.*

It is an act of self-love to refuse to see someone again who will eventually break your heart. Be among the women who have made heartfelt decisions out of a deep love for themselves, trusting that once they started making good choices, they would be able to have what they wanted. The choice to turn your back on what's not good for you may not be easy, because we are all susceptible to certain kinds of men—tall men, rich men, men with blue eyes, men who love dogs—and yet we can find men attractive who will *also* give us what we want. Remember: you are lovable and there is a man who wants to have a relationship with you. You don't need to sell yourself short. And besides—there's always another one coming!

## List #2: The Ten "Very Importants"

The ten "very importants" are exactly that—they are very important to you but they're not necessarily deal breakers. It may be very important that he own a house, for example, but if he fits almost all your other criteria and is currently renting an apartment, you might be able to overlook the fact that he isn't a homeowner. Or it may be important that he has a college degree, but if he is highly articulate, well read, and educated, it may not matter that he doesn't have his B.A. Yet you don't want to give in too easily on your "very importants." They are, after all, attributes that will make you happy.

If you go out with someone who has all six "musts" and many of the "very importants," he is a very good prospect. If he has three out of the ten "very importants," he might still work out, but your chances aren't as good. When you are having an openhearted relationship with yourself, you will want to give yourself the best chance of having a long-term, committed relationship with a man who has the qualities you want. To do that, you will want to choose the man who has a high number of "very importants."

Even if at first you're only a little attracted to a man who fits your lists, it would be worth your while to go out with him. You may well become more attracted to him in time, because he fits into your heartfelt lists of what you are looking for. Giving him a chance is a more self-loving thing to do than going out with the very appealing man who only has four "musts" and two "very importants."

## List #3: The Six "Must Nots"

The six "must nots" highlight what we call your pitfalls. Your pitfalls are your Achilles heel—the patterns you have that you've been hurt by. And even though you are now becoming aware of your patterns, it's human nature to be drawn to them. It would be helpful for you to refer to Chapter Seven and review your patterns as you create your "must not" list.

Having a "must not" list will help you stay awake enough to notice when you are approaching a pitfall. If your habit is being attracted to men who have substance abuse problems, you would want to put on your list "Must not be a substance abuser." If you have never been in relationship with a man who is a substance abuser, you wouldn't need to put that on your list. If you are attracted to men who flirt excessively, you will put on your list "Must not be a flirt"—and if you've never been with a man who flirts, that wouldn't be an item on your list.

When you go out with someone, you will want to be very much in the moment to help yourself be aware of your pitfalls. If you're not awake in the moment it is very easy to fall into an old pattern without realizing it. "He's not like all the others," you might think—without realizing that he is angry with women just like the others were. If you are awake, you will be present in the moment to realize that he is talking badly about his mother or his ex-wife. And later, when you sit down and compare him to your list, it will help you see you are approaching a pitfall.

### List #4: Unlimited "Wouldn't it be nice if..."

This list is for all the attributes that you'd enjoy a man having, but that are not "deal breakers," "very importants," or "must nots." They're the "extras," the things it would be great for him to have but that won't make or break your decision to get involved with him. You might think, "Wouldn't it be nice if he had a sporty car?" Another woman might have this on a different list. On *her* "Wouldn't it be nice if ..." list, she might write, "Wouldn't it be nice if he liked to sail?" You can have fun with this list and play with the picture of what you want, envisioning what you want your life to be like and what it will take to make you happy. Put as many things as you want on this list.

## Getting Clear

The clearer you get, the more you can magnetize the man you want toward you. Gaining clarity is a statement that says:

*"I am ready."*
*"I deserve to be happy."*
*"I know what will make me happy."*
*"I will receive him."*
*"I will cherish him."*
*"I will do my part of the work once he's here."*

Getting clear opens the way for what you want to show up. Fear often gets in the way of your clarity. Once you are sure, you won't let your fears stop you. Getting clear is a loving thing to do for yourself.

There is a really nice man out there who wants you to be clear so you can see him and be with him. Many women report that when they are clear about what they want, a man will just show up. In other words, because she was actively engaged in the process of getting ready and being clear about what she wanted, he appeared. It's like putting your order in for the relationship you want.

> *Getting clear opens the way for what you want to show up.*

You infinitely increase your odds of finding the right man by putting yourself out there. That might mean:

*Noticing available men every day*
*Being friendly*
*Agreeing to the blind dates your friends propose*
*Accepting dates even if he doesn't look like a Prince*
*Going to parties and social events*
*Doing charity work*

*Campaigning for people you believe in*
*Participating in your favorite sport or art form*
*Answering personal ads*
*Joining an Internet dating service*

Remember that while you are out there, you are also main-taining a loving relationship with yourself so you can stay strong and centered, not take things personally, and stick to what you know is good for you. Finding what's good for you means turning your back on what's not good for you. This may mean changing some of your patterns of selection, belief, and behavior.

**The reason you find one man more attrac-tive than another is often historical.**

If you've always gone for the tall blond men, you will want to be open to noticing and dating men who don't fit your pattern. The man who will treat you well, be a good father to your children, and cherish you forever might not be the one who is most appealing at first glance. Yet the reason you find one man more attractive than another is often historical. If you can get beyond that initial response and give him a chance, you may be surprised how you can begin to find someone handsome—even if he doesn't fit the pattern of what has always attracted you. A man can become extremely attractive when he cherishes you and treats you well.

*Your mother never told you...*
*that there was a systematic way you could*
*select the right man for you.*

**Checking Them Twice**

Your lists will be your best friends as you begin the process of meeting and getting to know men. Interviewing is a way of discovering how he fits in with what you want, which is contained in your lists. When you are out with a man, you will have in mind that you want to find out as much about him as possible. It doesn't mean you need to have a list of questions in front of you and fire them off at him or give him a one-page multiple-choice quiz. No one likes being grilled. But since you're a woman, you are naturally good at listening and you can find out a lot just by asking questions and really hearing what he has to say.

**A man can become extremely attractive when he cherishes you and treats you well.**

While you are having fun during your first couple of conversations, you might steer the subject toward one that's important to you and see how he reacts. If one of your "musts" is that he needs to be financially secure, you could talk about the stock market or the high rate of debt in the United States and see if it strikes a chord with him. If one of your "must nots" is that he must not be unfaithful, you could tell a story about a friend whose husband cheated on her and notice his response. If he thinks it's funny or takes the man's side, it would be a good clue that he takes the subject lightly. If he's mysterious and doesn't want to answer, be suspicious.

After your time together, even if you are really tired, you will want to record your general impressions. It is important to have your lists available in the place where you like to relax when you get home. If it's on the sofa, keep your lists on the coffee table. If it's on your bed, keep your lists on your night table. And with your lists you'll have a notebook to record everything you noticed about him. You can write about how he talked to you, how he treated the waiter, whether he was respectful to you and others, and how he spoke about his family, his friends, and his colleagues. Some things are more important than others, but you will want to write down as much as you can.

Once you've written about him in your notebook, get out your lists and look at the "musts." If he fits all six, it would be self-loving for you to see him again. If you don't have enough information about a "must," make notes so you know how to steer the next conversation you have with him. If he does not fit all six, *do not go out with him again.* You don't want to have your heart broken again, so save yourself the pain by simply not seeing him again.

To summarize:

1. *Buy a notebook to record your dating experiences.*
2. *Make your lists.*
3. *Read your lists before you go out, whether it's to a meeting place or on a date.*
4. *Put your lists and your notebook where you will land after you come home.*
5. *While you're out with him, be observant. Notice how he acts and what he says. Ask him a lot of questions about himself, and steer the conversation toward the subjects you want to find out about—and don't forget to have fun while you're doing it!*
6. *When you get home, record your impressions in your notebook. Write as many details about him as you can remember, in as objective a way as you can. If he's really your "type," remind yourself to stay awake.*
7. *Check what you know about him compared to your six "musts." You will come up with one of three conclusions:*
    a.) *He fits all six. In that case, see how he does with the "very importants" and the "must nots." If he's not your "type" but fits your six "musts," remind yourself it is a loving act to go out with him again.*
    b.) *He doesn't fit all six. Do not go out with him again.*
    c.) *You don't have enough information and you need to see him one or two more times before you can see how he fits for you.*
8. *Check your other lists: "Very Importants," "Pitfalls," and "Wouldn't it be nice if . . ."*

Being clear about what you want gives you power and allows you to relax. Then you can have fun, take care of yourself, and love yourself through the process of meeting men. Instead of waiting months or years to discover it's not going to work out, you can trust that you will have a very good idea after the first or second meeting. The challenge is to turn your back on him when you see he won't be the one for you. If you find him attractive it may be difficult to say no, yet loving yourself and knowing you deserve what you want will give you the strength to stop. If you don't stop seeing him now, it will probably end at some point—and with a much greater cost to you. Stopping now can save yourself heartbreak as well as months and years of your precious time. It is a statement that you are ready to have what is good for you.

Be self-loving as you choose a man.

*You can have fun, take care of yourself, and love yourself through the process of meeting men.*

*Your mother never told you . . .*
*that you could be very careful when looking for your mate.*

## The Gifts They Gave Themselves

The following are true stories of women who used "Conscious Choosing" with great success. We hope you will be inspired.

### Victoria

Victoria took the "Having What You Want With a Man" Workshop shortly after turning forty-two—with dramatic results.

"After years of swinging back and forth between wanting a husband and family and wanting to stay single, the Workshop opened the way for me to get married," she says. "I got very clear and very focused. By the end of the weekend I knew I was ready to get married soon and I wanted a man who would be a good husband and father.

"I took everything Marilyn said very seriously. I made my lists and created a dating notebook. I joined a dating service, answered personal ads, and went to singles' events. I made dating into a second job. I was just as focused and motivated about finding a man as I was about getting the next big contract at work. In fact, for over two months I went out with a different man nearly every night of the week.

"I got very good at interviewing men to find out if they wanted the same things I wanted, and if they would be a good match for me or not. It's amazing how efficient I became. Instead of having to draw out a relationship for months before figuring out if he was the one, I could know right away. A man who drinks is one of my pitfalls, so if a man had more than two drinks while we were together, I knew I didn't want to see him again.

"I was very firm with myself about not seeing a man again if I knew he wasn't what I wanted—even if he was attractive. I had a lot of first dates and only a few second dates. After a couple of months of actively dating, I met Frank, the man I was pretty sure I wanted to marry. He fit all my requirements: he was a member of my religion, financially secure, around my age, didn't have any children from his former marriage, and wanted to get married and adopt children.

"Frank and I both felt that at our age, there was no time to waste. Once we were both certain, we started planning our wedding. We got married in July—seven months after I took the Workshop. It was truly amazing. Now we are very happy and have adopted two children from China. I have everything I wanted."

## Heather

Heather took the Workshop as a last resort after years of heartbreak. She had a history of six- to eight-month relationships that ended badly, and she had run out of hope that she could ever have what she wanted with a man. She didn't really believe the Workshop would help her, but she figured she had nothing to lose.

"I was pretty resistant to a lot of the information and I'm sure I was holding back. But it had a profound effect on me nonetheless—one that didn't surface in my consciousness until over a year later," Heather explains.

"I met Matt not long after the Workshop and we got pretty serious after a few months. I thought, 'Well, maybe I did get something out of the weekend after all.' I could tell that I was more open and heartfelt with him than I'd ever been before, and I thought maybe this would be the one. After we'd been together for a few months, we drove to Philadelphia so I could introduce Matt to my parents. I was really excited for them to meet him, especially my mother. She'd never liked any of my boyfriends much, but I was sure this time it would be different.

"The weekend was a disaster. My mother was her usual gracious self, but she kept asking Matt pointed questions, then raising her eyebrows when he answered. She made him feel really uncomfortable, and when I confronted her about it she just started telling me how he wasn't good enough for me, he didn't make enough money, he wasn't cultured enough, and on and on. By the time we left Philadelphia, Matt and I were at each other's throats from the tension—and not long afterward we broke up.

"The breakup was really hard on me because I had really been hopeful about our relationship. I went into a depression for a while, thinking I would never have what I wanted. Then something told me to look back over my notebook from the course. Nothing really popped out at me until I looked at the section on patterns—then it hit me like a lightning bolt!

"I saw that I had a pattern of my relationships ending soon after I introduced the man to my mother, usually between five and seven months into it. And I realized that my mother's criticism of the men I brought home caused me to react against them, even though actually I disagreed with my mother. I was taking on her criticism and I would literally start to hear her voice in my head. So I saw that introducing a man to my mother was my pitfall. If

I were ever going to get married I knew I would have to keep the man away from my mother until I had a ring on my finger—and even then I'd have to be very careful.

"Recognizing my pitfall was huge for me. I was so grateful for having the wisdom to review what I learned despite my resistance. When I met Eric I made sure to stay awake and aware, not only to avoid discussing him in any way with my mother but to avoid my mother's critical voice taking over my own thoughts. And it worked! We got married two years ago and I've never been happier. When my mother starts trying to talk to me about Eric, I just tell her gently that I don't want to discuss it. And she is starting to respect that and to respect me more as a person, I can tell. I never expected that taking care of myself would not only help me have what I want with a man, but help my relationship with my mother as well."

### Stephanie

Stephanie met Joaquin on a singles trip to Costa Rica. She'd gotten up the nerve to take the trip after the Workshop, but she didn't really expect to meet anyone. Her attraction to Joaquin took her by surprise. She enjoyed the fact that he spoke fluent Spanish and could interpret for her when they were bargaining for gifts in the marketplace or ordering seafood at a restaurant. Still, she felt a lot of resistance and made sure to be in a group of people every time she was with him. She gently rebuffed his overtures and told him she wanted to be just friends.

"I thought it was just a vacation romance, and I didn't want to get hurt," Stephanie says. "I was sure that once we were back in the United States he would forget all about me. After all, he lived in California and I lived in Illinois. I didn't want to fall into another intense, fast-moving relationship the way I had a pattern of doing. I was determined that the next time I got involved with a man would be the last—meaning, I would spend the rest of my life with him.

"I went on with my life when I got home, thinking about Joaquin once in a while but not dwelling on him—so I was very surprised to get a call from him a few weeks later. He told me he had to come to Chicago on business the following week and he'd like to see me. I was a little apprehensive, but I agreed to meet him for dinner.

"We really had a fabulous time, and I started taking Joaquin more seriously after that. He was actively pursuing me, calling me several times a week and wanting to make further plans to get together. Eventually I agreed to visit him in Los Angeles, and again we had a wonderful time. But when Joaquin started talking about one of us moving so we could be closer together, I balked. I realized I was happy with how things were for the time being. I made it clear to him that I wanted to take it slowly, that I needed to maintain my own life in Illinois and that I'd been hurt too many times before by rushing into things.

"Joaquin agreed to take it slowly, and we continued having a long-distance relationship for two years. Finally I agreed to marry him, and it's been wonderful. Joaquin moved his business to Chicago, where he'd always done a lot of business anyway, and we've been married for nearly five years now. I know that the reason it worked was that I had enough love for myself to honor my need to take it slowly, rather than saying yes right away out of fear that he'd lose interest. I trusted my instincts and it worked out better than I could have imagined."

### Melinda

When Melinda came to Life Works she was involved in an intense relationship with Herb, an emergency room physician. She and Herb argued often, and their interactions almost always involved a high level of stress.

"I was exhausted," admits Melinda. "I'd been seeing Herb for nearly three years, and the relationship was taking a lot out of me. Herb didn't like it that I was so busy with my career and my charities. I guess he felt threatened, and he made it really hard on me.

"After about a year of serious work on myself, I realized that my relationship with Herb could only go so far. I was trying to own my part, not be a victim, be softer with him, and open my heart to both of us. But the dynamics of our relationship were already so charged that my shifts made very little difference in the overall picture. I felt desperate, knowing I needed to turn my back on this unhealthy relationship and yet frightened to death that I'd never find another man. I was nearing my fifties, and I was terrified of growing old alone.

"Finally after a particularly draining evening with Herb, I knew I had to make a choice to leave. I had to do it because I loved myself and I knew I deserved better. So I broke off this four-year relationship, which was one of the hardest things I've ever done in my life.

"Thank goodness I had the support of the women at Life Works and my friends, all of whom were relieved I'd finally ended it. They'd seen how much it took out of me. Being single after so long was really difficult for a while, but I never doubted I'd done the right thing for myself. I was able to love myself enough to do the things that nurtured me through the hard part, and when I started getting gripped about being alone I just asked myself, 'What's the most loving thing I can do for myself now?' That question helped to ground me and to keep me from picking up the phone and calling Herb.

"Eight months after ending my 'last worst relationship,' as Marilyn calls it, I met Justin at one of the Life Works get-togethers. It hadn't really occurred to me that I'd meet someone interesting—I went mostly to get out of the house and know I was doing something instead of sitting home feeling sorry for myself. But Justin had all the qualities I wanted in a man and he was also very committed to working on himself. Now we're married and my life is better than I ever could have anticipated. I never would have gotten here if I hadn't had the courage to turn my back on what wasn't good for me. And I am forever grateful that I did. Now I know I can count on myself to take care of myself."

## Alexis

Alexis was always attracted to men with broad shoulders, thick wavy hair, and impeccable taste in clothes. She kept herself fit and meticulously groomed, and was never short of handsome, well-dressed admirers. Yet in her early thirties Alexis realized that what she wanted more than anything was to start a family. The men she was accustomed to dating weren't necessarily the fatherly type, and when she would bring up her desire to have children they would respond less than enthusiastically.

"I couldn't figure out why I couldn't find a man who wanted to be a father to my children," says Alexis. "I always had at least one man interested in me, but none of them seemed like really good prospects once I got to know them better. I would moan about them to my friend Will, who was always there for me with a sympathetic ear. He'd take me out for pizza and beer, listen to my troubles sympathetically, and support me wholeheartedly, telling me how great I was and how lucky any man would be to have me. But things weren't improving, so I knew I had to take some action. My biological clock was ticking.

"Finally I signed up for the Workshop and it helped me understand that I'd been picking men based on physical criteria rather than on what was really important to me. I made my lists of what I wanted in a man and determined to choose better for myself in future. I opened myself to noticing different kinds of men than the ones I'd always gone for, and I started dating all sorts of people. Still, though, nothing seemed quite right. I was still crying in my beer to Will on a weekly basis.

"One day Molly, one of the women I'd met at Life Works, asked me, 'Why don't you date Will? It sounds like he really cares about you.'

"'Will?' I was astonished. Will had been my friend forever, and it had never crossed my mind that he could be a prospect. He was a little shorter than me and he was balding. He was a contractor and wore plaid shirts and jeans—he was just such a regular *guy*. He wasn't distinguished like the men I'd been attracted to. And besides, he was my friend.

"Molly's question stuck in my head, though. I had been noticing new kinds of men since the Workshop, and now I made myself look at Will as a man instead of as my personal teddy bear. The more I thought about it, the more I realized that Will had all the qualities I wanted in a man—and more. I remembered that many women found him attractive. He was kind, thoughtful, generous, and supportive. He was self-employed, had plenty of money, and wanted a wife and kids. He had a good relationship with his family and volunteered at the local soup kitchen once a week.

"The next time I saw Will, I asked him playfully what he would say if I asked him out. I had no idea whether or not he was attracted to me or whether he, too, thought of me as just a buddy.

"'You want to ask me out?' he asked, staring at me in disbelief.

"I thought his disbelief meant that he'd never thought of me that way, and I was really embarrassed.

"'Forget it, it was just a joke,' I mumbled.

"I was afraid to meet his eyes, but when I did I saw that he looked crestfallen. And suddenly I was filled with this incredible feeling of relief and joy! I knew then that Will wanted to be with me, and I knew we would have a family together. It was the best moment of my life. And if I hadn't been open to giving myself what I deeply wanted, it never would have happened, I'm sure. I would have ended up with some really well dressed but cold man who didn't want kids, and I'd be miserable. Instead, I'm married to the greatest guy in the world and I'm pregnant with our third child."

*Your mother never told you...*
*how grateful you'd be when you found a great*
*man.*

*T*hink about...

 What a "day in the life of my marriage" would be like. Have it be a realistic, ordinary day and see it in detail.

*The exercises for Chapter Twelve can be found on page 272.*

# Chapter Thirteen

# Looking Forward

Ask any married woman about the day she met her husband and she will probably be able to describe it in detail. She'll get a faraway look in her eye and launch into a description. "Oh yes—I remember it was a really gloomy day, so when I went out to go shopping, I brought my yellow umbrella. I was feeling good despite the clouds, swinging along in my red dress and enjoying catching my reflection in shop windows. All of a sudden there was a huge clap of thunder and it started raining cats and dogs. I managed to get my umbrella up but immediately the wind blew it inside out. I got drenched! Oh, it was a mess."

She'll shake her head, a smile on her face. "I started running, I knew there was a coffee shop up ahead where I could take shelter. I burst in through the door, dripping all over the floor. Everyone in the place turned to look at me and I was really embarrassed. I knew my hair was all straggly and my dress was clinging to me. Well, this cute guy came over as I was standing in line. 'Let me buy you a cup of coffee,' he said. 'You look like you could use it.' He came and sat with me, even brought me napkins so I could dry off a little. We started chatting away like old friends—and next thing I knew, I was giving him my phone number!"

Why does she remember the meeting in such detail? Because it turned out to be a very important moment in her life. Yet if you ask her about the day before she met her husband, she will likely draw a blank. "The day before we met? I don't remember," she might say. "I guess it was just an ordinary day."

No one remembers the day before they met their mate. It was probably a day like any other with its tasks, challenges, and joys. It was probably a day a lot like today, in fact. A day in which at some point you feel a yearning to meet a man who will be a loving, supportive, kind, caring partner. A day in which you may be experiencing impatience, and wondering when it's going to happen. A day in which you can trust that it will happen when you are ready.

*No one remembers the day before they met their mate.*

It will happen—it's just a matter of time. A womanly outlook on life is optimistic, knowing that all the things we desire are coming our way. When we're optimistic we create room for what we want to come toward us. At Life Works we have seen it happen for enough women that we know it will happen for you when it's time. While you are developing your relationship with yourself, nurturing yourself, accepting yourself, giving yourself good things, and opening your heart to yourself, you are preparing the space for him to come into your life, too. It may happen tomorrow, or it may be months or years before you're ready to meet him. Knowing that it's just a matter of time can allow you to relax and be patient with yourself. It can't happen until you are ready—and it's worth taking the time to prepare for it.

*There is a big difference between waiting for a Prince and preparing yourself for a real relationship with a real man.*

*Your mother never told you. . .*
    *that whatever you want can happen—it's just*
    *a matter of time.*

# Ready?

There is a big difference between waiting for a Prince and preparing yourself for a *real* relationship with a *real* man. Waiting for a Prince is passive—staring out windows, singing to yourself "Someday my Prince will come," watching *Casablanca* over and over. When you're yearning to meet a *real* man who can make you happy, there are things you can *be* and things you can *do* that will have you be ready when he walks around the corner.

## Things to be:

| | |
|---|---|
| *Awake* | Remembering your history. |
| *Aware* | Noticing your old beliefs when they creep up on you. |
| *Listening* | Tuning in to your hidden conversations. |
| *Tolerant* | Living with the discomfort of change. |
| *Watchful* | Taking care not to repeat patterns or step into pitfalls. |
| *Careful* | Choosing well for yourself. |
| *Patient* | Letting things take the time they take. |
| *Openhearted* | Loving yourself, forgiving yourself, and being easy with yourself. |
| *Kind* | Not beating yourself up, blaming yourself, or criticizing yourself. |
| *Accepting* | You are human, you are living in a trial-and-error universe, and you are doing the best you can. |
| *Grateful* | Thankful for your unique gifts, talents, desires, and strengths |
| *Generous* | Giving yourself good things. |
| *Fun* | Enjoying yourself and your life right now. |
| *Expectant* | Looking forward to the good relationship you deserve. |
| *Optimistic* | Knowing that it's all going to happen, it's just a matter of time. |

Isn't it great to know you are already starting to be ready to meet the man you want? Every time you take care of yourself in

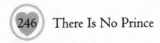

a new way, open your heart to yourself a little more, give yourself what you want, are easy with yourself, and make a decision to choose something that's good for you—you are preparing for having what you desire. Congratulations!

While you are making room for him by *being* new ways, you can also *do* things that will invite him into your life.

*Isn't it great to know you are already starting to be ready to meet the man you want?*

### Things to do:

*Create the living space you want.* Does your house or apartment reflect who you are right now? Taking a look around your living space can give you a lot of clues about yourself. Imagine being a man coming in for the first time. What does your place say about you? It could be saying any of the following;

"I'm not really settled in here. I'm just passing through—that's why all the boxes still aren't unpacked."

*Silent message: "I'm waiting for a Prince to take me to his castle."*

"I'm too busy to spend much time at home."

*Silent message: "I don't have time for a relationship."*

"I create a nurturing space for myself."

*Silent message: "I care about myself enough to have what I want."*

"I can't be bothered to do housework."

*Silent message: "I don't take care of myself well."*

"I furnish my place with pieces that are important to me."

*Silent message: "I give myself good things."*

"Everything has to be exactly in its place."

*Silent message: "I'm not willing to let someone else share my space."*

"I want people to feel comfortable here."

*Silent message: "I have room for others in my life."*

"I haven't redecorated since college."

*Silent message: "I'm not ready for a grown-up relationship."*

If your home doesn't reflect who you are now, it would be worth it for you to take some time to focus on creating a space that says what you want it to say about you. Devote some time to imagining how you want a man to respond to your home. Men will unconsciously respond to your surroundings as a clue to who you are and what you are ready to have in your life.

**Buy clothes that make you feel wonderful.** When you meet someone or go out with him, you want to feel as confident and attractive as possible. Going through your closet is a good way to weed out the clothes that might make you feel dowdy, unappealing, or uncomfortable. You'll want to have several outfits on hand that you'll feel great in. When you go out with a man, it's helpful to bear in mind a few guidelines about clothes:

*Steer clear of business suits. You are meeting your husband not making a deal.*

*Wear softer fabrics and brighter colors.*

*Make sure you feel totally comfortable and unselfconscious.*

**Be aware of the message your clothes are giving out.** If you wear something too sexy, you might be giving off the wrong message—and if you wear something too masculine, you also might be giving off the wrong message. You probably don't want him to think you're either "easy" or "one of the guys." Above all, make sure you feel fabulous in what you're wearing. When you feel great you'll give off a confident glow—and even if he doesn't turn out to be what you want, you'll know you gave it your best shot.

**Have ingredients for a quick meal in the house.** There's truth in the old saying, "The way to a man's heart is through his stomach." Having some good, easy-to-prepare food in the fridge is a great way to show you're ready to have someone in your life. If you hate to cook, have some gourmet takeout available in the freezer. He'll be grateful if you're both hungry after the movie and you can whip up some pasta or chicken salad sandwiches. And having a selection of drinks to offer is also a good idea. He will appreciate your foresight. Men love to be fed!

*Know places to eat out and things to do on a date.* Since he wants you to be happy, he might want you to pick the place to go or the activities to do. If you can quickly refer to a mental list of restaurants you like, movies that you want to see, and other entertainment options, it will make things go a lot smoother for you if he hasn't already picked out what to do.

Preparing to have men enter your life is like prepping for a presentation at work or buying the ingredients when you're going to bake a cake. It's simply being ready for the upcoming situation. Conscious choosing doesn't mean being different from how you are—it means being more of who you are. As a woman, you are naturally good at planning for the future and knowing how to

> Conscious choosing doesn't mean being different from how you are—it means being more of who you are.

have things run smoothly. You will enjoy the process of getting ready to meet the man you want if you use your natural abilities to make dating an easier and more pleasurable process.

*Your mother never told you...*
   *that dating would go better when you are more fully yourself.*

## Set?

When you write in your notebook after a meeting with a man, take a moment to see if he fits into what you envision about your future. Can you picture him going to museums with you, picking the kids up from school, rubbing your feet after a long day, or helping you hoe the garden? If you can't picture him by your side supporting you in what you want to do, there's a good chance he doesn't fit. It's not foolproof, but your powers of envisioning are very strong. When you tap into them as a tool to help you create the life you want, it's amazing what can happen.

***

Now that you are free from being entranced by your childhood influences, you can create a picture for yourself that is authentic for you right now.

***

When you envision something it's like running your own private movie for yourself or taking a snapshot of your future. And the great thing about living at this moment in history is that for the first time women really do have the freedom to create the picture we want.

Without realizing it, it's possible that you are living with an old picture of the future you desire—one that you formed when you were five, twelve, or twenty-two, or one that comes from your mother, your aunt, or your grandmother. And that picture was influenced by the history you lived through, the beliefs you formed, the relationship you had with yourself, the patterns you created, and the choices you made. Now that you are free from being entranced by your childhood influences, you can create a picture for yourself that is authentic for you right now.

Like the women whose stories you read in the last chapter, what you want will show up once you are absolutely clear. Victoria got clear that she was ready to be married, then approached dating as a serious path to meeting the right man. Stephanie ended up taking the opposite path when she met the right man and *then* took all the time she needed to get clear. Alexis had to identify what she didn't want with other men before she could clear the way for what she *did* want with the man who'd been there all along. Heather got clear that she had to find a man without her mother's input, and Melinda clearly saw that she had to turn her back on the relationship that

***

Remind yourself of your true desires and keep your arms open, ready to receive what is coming your way.

***

There Is No Prince

wasn't good for her in order to have one that would be good for her.

There may be times when you have to encourage yourself to keep awake and keep moving toward what you want. You are worth the time, attention, and energy it takes. Remind yourself of your true desires and keep your arms open, ready to receive what is coming your way. Don't give up on yourself and him. Remember he's out there looking for you, too.

**It will happen, it's just a matter of time.**

The clearer you get about what you want, the more in focus your picture will be. And the sharper the picture, the more easily you will attract into your life what you desire. The more specific you can be, the better. The following practices can help you have the future you want:

1. *Allow yourself some private space and time to reflect on what you've learned about yourself*
2. *Go over your lists*
3. *Picture how you want a day in your life to be and how you want a year in your life to be*
4. *Write about what you want*
5. *Create a collage of pictures that illustrate what you want and hang it on the wall*
6. *If there are things you're not clear about, hold a space for them in your heart and leave space for them in your writings and collage*

*ℒ♥*

We have the free-dom to create the relationships we want and have the lives we dream of.

*ℒ♥*

How does a man fit into the future you envision? Maybe he travels a lot so you can still have time on your own, or maybe you both work at home together. Perhaps he will have a high-powered career so you can care for the children, or maybe you'll both work part-time so you can share the responsibility of raising a family. However it works for you, you can have the future and the relationship that fits you. You're fortunate to be living at a unique point in history when we have the freedom to create the relationships we want and have the lives we dream of.

*Your mother never told you. . .*
    *that you could envision your future.*

**Go!**

Imagine that now you have your reward for all the work you've done—a man who can love you for who you are and support you in whatever life brings toward you. What will it be like as you get into a relationship with this man you have chosen carefully? Luckily, most of it is up to you.

You can design the relationship you want because you have opened your heart to yourself. Knowing your heartfelt desires has allowed you to envision what you want. You have given yourself the time to choose, through a thoughtful process of interviewing and selection that is different from how you've done it in the past. You have cared enough about your happiness to make sure you have stayed awake and aware in the moment, avoided old patterns, and turned your back on what is not good for you. You have envisioned how you want your life to be—and now you can have it.

**There are as many ways of being together as there are couples.**

We are fortunate to be living in a time when there is no "is-ness" about relationships. It used to be that relationships meant marriage, and marriage meant he went out to work and she stayed home. It can still mean that if that is what you want—and if you want something entirely different you can create it. No two relationships are the same. You can get inspiration from other people's relationships, molding the parts you like into what will work well for you—and adding your own unique twists. There are as many ways of being together as there are couples.

Choosing the right man for you means you have the opportunity to create the right relationship for you. Because he fits all your "musts" and most of your "very importants," you know he wants the same things from life that you do. He will support you in your desires and cheer you on as you accomplish them. When you go into the relationship knowing it is a work in progress, you can expect that it will transform as you both continue to grow and expand.

*When you go into the relationship knowing it is a work in progress, you can expect that it will transform as you both continue to grow and expand.*

As you begin developing the rich, juicy, satisfying relationship you want, there are a few things it will help you to remember.

Your relationship can be divine when you're willing to...

*Keep your heart open to yourself*

*Take time to nurture your relationship with yourself*

*Recognize your patterns and see when you are repeating something from your history*

*Open your heart to him*

*Accept that you are both human*

*Forgive yourself for your mistakes*

*Forgive him for his mistakes*

*Continue to give yourself good things*

*Give yourself the benefit of the doubt*

*Give him the benefit of the doubt*

*Do things differently from how you've done them in the past*

*Understand and accept who he is*

*Be willing to do what works*

*Stay out of his belly button*
*Help him know what to do to make you happy*
*Be a leader in relationship*
*Admit you're wrong when you're wrong*
*Own your part in what is happening*
*Don't take things personally*
*Have your own authentic life*
*Tolerate feeling bad so a good thing can happen*
*Remember why you love him*
*Relax and have fun!*

Like the women whose stories you've read, you *can* have what you want with a man. You can fulfill your heartfelt desires and you can have happiness. You are preparing the way by loving yourself enough to let it take the time it takes and trusting that it will happen. It's just a matter of time. Who knows?—he may be coming around the corner right now.

*Your mother never told you. . .*
  *that you can create a relationship that fits you.*

*Think about. . .*

 **Living from "It will happen, it's just a matter of time."**

*The exercises for Chapter Thirteen can be found on page 274.*

Today may be the day
before you meet your husband.

# AFTERWORD

"People in relationship are like two rough stones. When you rub them together long enough and hard enough, they become two smooth stones." With these words, Swami Satchidananda gives us a new way to think about relationships.

We each bring our own rough edges into a relationship—old hurts that have not been healed, lack of self-love, and beliefs and patterns of behavior that need attention. And when our rough edges jostle his, it can be painful—especially because we think there shouldn't be any rough edges. We've been led to believe that when we meet our Prince it will be easy to ride off into the sunset with him, and the problems we've had in other relationships simply won't exist. It's no wonder we think there's something wrong when the rough edges start colliding!

In fact, it's impossible to have a committed relationship without bumping into each other occasionally, or maybe even daily. When we can recognize the rough spots as places that need to be healed rather than as insurmountable problems, we can work together to smooth our stones. We can acknowledge our rough spots and accept his. And knowing that it smoothes the edges each time we bump against each other helps keep us optimistic.

Seeing yourself and the man you choose as two rough stones helps you see your relationship as a place for learning. You can view it as a laboratory where you can experiment with acceptance, compassion, negotiation, responsibility, patience, and love. As your stones rub together, you share the intimate process of smoothing out the bumps. Instead of tearing you apart, the collisions can bring you closer together and help you achieve your potential as individuals and as a couple. After years of smoothing the edges, you will fit together easily and will joyfully tumble through the river of life.

# Quick Help
# For Having What You Want

## Things to remember about yourself

What you expect is what you get.

Healing your history lets your future be different from your past.

Your beliefs are not the truth.

You can create new beliefs that allow you to have what you want.

Tuning in to your hidden conversations helps you understand why you have what you have.

Your relationship with yourself is the most important one you'll ever have.

Staying awake and aware in the moment is a way to have things be different.

Tolerating your feelings allows things to change.

You are human and you make mistakes.

Making new choices means turning your back on what's not good for you.

Forgiving yourself opens your heart to accepting more love.

You have patterns of selection, belief, and behavior.

You will be drawn to repeat your patterns even if you are aware of them.

You have commitment issues, too.

Owning your part gives you your power back.

Be aware of being critical and hard to please.

Your tone of voice matters.

Give him the problem he gives you.

It works best for you to go first.

You are the source of the relationship.

You are more complicated than he is.

You have the power to attract the man and the relationship you want.


## Things to remember about him

He is not a Prince.

He was not put on the planet to make your life work.

His ego is fragile and he gets hurt easily.

His behavior is often a cover for his sensitivity.

When he feels vulnerable he will resist going first.

He needs to feel safe.

He is more attached to you than you are to him.

He needs to be known by you.

He is a romantic but shows it only when he knows you will receive it.

He is psychic. He knows when something is wrong and he will unconsciously react to it.

He hides his tender feelings.

He lives in the present.

He is simpler than you are.

He is in awe of you.

He wants to be your hero.

He forgets.

His sense of time is different from yours.

He is not doing it to hurt you.

When he is hurt he does "bad boy" things.

He wants you as much as you want him.

He wants to please you.

He needs you to treat him well so he can please you.

He needs positive, loving attention...

...and so do you!

# Exercises

## INTRODUCTION

The following exercises were designed to support you in making the material in this book real to you. They are designed to be done as you finish the chapters, as a way of supporting yourself further as you shift your life from where it is now to where you want it to be. Do not feel that you have to do them all. You can pick and choose as you like, and take them at your own pace. It may be useful to read the book through once and then read each chapter again as you do the exercises.

Some of these can be done at first glance. Others may take some consideration and some time. Feel free to do the exercises as many times as will serve you. Let the answers drop onto the page without censoring them. And expect to be surprised. Please allow the responses to take the time they need. You are worth it.

Since this work and its results can be very subtle, you may not see obvious changes right away. We believe that the smallest shift is a leap into the future because change is made from an accumulation of small steps.

We have selected several films as suggestions for viewing with each chapter. They are designed to inspire, enrich, and illuminate what you will be thinking about as you move through the book. We intend for them to provide experiences of the relationship dilemma, the process of change, and the triumph of the human spirit.

If you have any films to add to this list, please email us with your suggestions to be reviewed for future editions.

Enjoy yourself and relax with a good movie.

### Exercise

You can start to get clear about what you want right now by asking yourself:

**"What do I want a man for?"**

You'll want to refer to your answers to this question as you go through the book, so it's a good idea to write the question at the top of the page in your notebook. You can add to the list later if you want to, but don't be surprised if it's not too long. Chances are, what you want a man for is actually less complicated than you thought. Getting clear about what you want a man for will prepare the way for you to gain a deeper understanding of why you've had what you've had—and how to go about having something different.

*Terms of Endearment*
*Class Action*
*Dangerous Beauty*
*The Contender*

## CHAPTER ONE: THERE IS NO PRINCE

**Exercises**

1. Reflect on the statement, "There is No Prince." What can happen for you now that you know there is No Prince. Take notes on your thoughts and feelings.

2. Notice men who do not fit your picture of the Prince. For each man, ask yourself honestly, "What might women see in him?"

3. Like Oona, what information have you been given that now seems like "the wrong information"?

*Snow White*
*Cinderella*
*Sleeping Beauty*
*Lady and the Tramp*
*Little Mermaid*

# CHAPTER TWO: What You Were Taught About Men

**Exercises**

1. Make a lists of movies, televisions shows, books, and songs that strongly influenced you as a child and young adult.

   > Think about how you were influenced by them.
   > What did they teach you about how life *should* be?
   > Rent some of the movies and see what you learned.

2. Begin a list of things your mother never told you. Add to this list as you read the book.

3. What did you learn to expect based on your parents' relationship?

4. What new expectations could you form that would work better?

5. Create a chronological list of significant relationships you've had with men.

*Sixteen Candles*
*Witness*
*Postcards From the Edge*
*Welcome to the Dollhouse*

# CHAPTER THREE: The Beliefs You Formed

## Exercises

1. Take your list of movies, television shows, books, and songs from Chapter Two and see what beliefs you formed based on them.

2. List some of the messages you picked up from advertising. What beliefs do you think you formed based on these ads?

3. Take your answer to question 4 from the previous chapter and see what beliefs you formed based on the expectations set up by your parents' relationship.

4. Game of Make Believe:

    Make a list of things you believe that are in the way of having the relationship you want. Why do you think you formed those beliefs?

    An example would be, "I believe all men will leave because Daddy left Mommy."

5. Think about what beliefs you'd like to live from that would support you in having the relationship you want.

    Write them down.

6. Choose one belief and take it through the "Four Steps to Shifting a Belief."

*South Pacific*
*The King & I*
*Good Bye Girl*

# CHAPTER FOUR: Promises You Made

**Exercises**

1. The following open-ended sentences are designed to help you discover your hidden conversations about love and relationships. Write each sentence on a separate page of your notebook and write the responses underneath it. Let yourself finish each sentence at least ten times, and try not to censor what comes out. It may help to speak the sentence and finish it, seeing what drops out of your mouth. Be prepared to be surprised!

   What is hard about marriage is...

   All marriages...

2. Reflect on the following possible hidden conversations.
   a) If I were in a great relationship, my mother would feel...
   b) If I were in a great relationship, my father would feel...
   c) Can a man be more special than my father? If not, why can't he be more special?
   d) Am I living out my mother's fantasy of what an independent life could have been? If yes, how?
   e) Am I making sure my parents appear to others as if they did *not* do a good job raising me?

3. Notice when you are doing things that are not consistent with having what you want in a relationship. Reflect on what hidden conversation might have you doing that. Take notes.

4. The hidden conversations I notice/have are...

   What I can do to heal them is...

*Breakfast at Tiffany's*
*Mother*
*The Kid*

# CHAPTER FIVE: Finding a Man Begins With…

## Exercises

1. Write the question, "What is the most loving thing I can do for myself now?" on a piece of paper and tape it to your fridge or your bathroom mirror. Remember to ask yourself the question as often as possible.

2. What would it be like if you lived from knowing there is nothing wrong with you? Write your responses.

   Experiment by going for a day, then a week, without allowing yourself to ask, "What is wrong with me?" When something isn't going your way, you can't respond with "There's something wrong with me." See how that feels.

3. Heart workout:

   Notice when your heart is open, then close it a little.

   Notice when it is closed, and open it a little.

   Notice when someone else is closing or opening their heart.

   Write about how it feels to know that you can have your heart be as open or as closed as you want.

4. Notice even the smallest ways you are loving yourself.

   Enjoy yourself.

5. Notice how other people treat you when you are loving yourself.

*Working Girl*
*Sabrina*
*Ever After*

# CHAPTER SIX: Feeling Bad So a Good Thing Can Happen

**Exercises**

1. Notice when you feel compelled to take an action that is not good for you (for example, when you have phone-in-hand disease).

    See if you can tolerate the feeling you are having for a while before taking any action.

    Build a practice of using the Seven Steps to Tolerating Feelings.

    Take notes on yourself.

2. Allow yourself to envision what you would like to move toward as you begin making new choices.

3. Keep a list of what you might have to turn your back on in order to have what you really want with a man.

*African Queen*
*Moonstruck*
*Broadcast News*

# CHAPTER SEVEN: Having Your Future Be Different From the Past

## Exercises

1. Look through the list of men who were significant to you.

    What are your patterns of selection?

    What are your patterns of belief?

    What are your patterns of behavior?

    What anniversaries do you have?

2. Try this out:

    Every day for a week, notice three men you may never have noticed as men before.

    What happens when you start noticing different men?

    Take notes.

3. Reflect on the patterns you would like to have.

    Write them down.

4. Who do you know who has what you want?

    What can you learn from her?

    Take notes.

*Baby Boom*
*Once Around*
*Groundhog Day*

# CHAPTER EIGHT: Owning Your Part

**Exercises**

1. Respond to the next two questions many times, and write them in your notebook.

   > What would you like to change about you and relationship?

   > What part of that dilemma can you own?

   > Allow yourself to feel relief and experience more power.

2. Reflect on your need for distance.

   > Take notes.

3. Reflect on your feelings about commitment.

   > Take notes.

*Shirley Valentine*
*An American President*
*Chocolat*

# CHAPTER NINE: Understanding a Few Things About Men

**Exercises**

1. What would life be like if you accepted men the way they are?

2. Make a list of "princely" characteristics of the men who have been in your life.

3. What do you notice about how men are that you understand in a different way now?

4. Reflect on what you need in order to create an environment for a man to give you what you want?
   Take notes.

*The Best Years of Our Lives*
*Marty*
*Lonely Guy*
*Three Men and a Baby*
*Swingers*
*The Tao of Steve*

# CHAPTER TEN: He'll Be Your Hero If You Let Him

**Exercises**

    Reflect and write about each phrase below one at a time.
        Take your time.
    What would life be like if you knew...
        men want to make you happy?
        you are the keeper of the relationship?
        if you go first he will follow?
        men want you to be strong and have your own life?
        men get more attached to you than you do to them?
        a man wants to be known, understood, and
            appreciated?

*Say Anything*
*Pretty Woman*
*Enchanted April*

**CHAPTER ELEVEN:** Knowing Your Power

I. Notice times you are being powerful in a female way...
> Nurturing
> Cooperating
> Communicating
> Being tender
> Empowering
> Knowing
> Creating
> Envisioning
> Being open
> Being receptive

2. Think of times in all your past relationships when you were being powerful, even if you didn't recognize it at the time.
> Take notes.

3. In what ways are you powerful? Take notes.
> In what ways are you powerful in relationships? Take notes.

4. Think of a fun way to use your power.
> Do it.

*Gigi*
*Steel Magnolias*
*Antonia's Line*
*Erin Brockovich*

## CHAPTER TWELVE: The Man You Want Is Out There

**Exercises**

Make your lists.

Take your time.

Perhaps write in pencil so you can reflect on which list
certain characteristics belong.

Create your final lists in pen.

What I want a man for?

"Must" list:

1.
2.
3.
4.
5.
6.

"Very Important" list

1.
2.
3.
4.
5.
6.
7.
8.
9.
10.

"Must Not" list—Pitfalls

   1.

   2.

   3.

   4.

   5.

   6.


"Wouldn't it be nice if..." list
Unlimited




*Pretty in Pink*
*Crossing Delancey*
*Only You*

# CHAPTER THIRTEEN: Looking Forward

**Exercises**

Consider and write your responses.

1. What would it be like if, as you look for your man, you know "it will happen, it's just a matter of time"?

2. What do you need to do to have:
   a) Your home ready?
   b) Your wardrobe ready?
   c) Refreshments ready?
          ... so you feel unselfconscious and prepared.
   d) What of the above are you ready to do now?

3. Write a list of restaurants you like in many price ranges and a list of things you want to do. Keep it current.

4. Envision your future. See yourself doing things you enjoy. Take notes.

*The Philadelphia Story*
*An Officer and a Gentleman*
*Accidental Tourist*
*Defending Your Life*
*Sleepless in Seattle*

# ADDITIONAL RESOURCES:
# BOOKS AND WEB SITES

## Books

Gray, John, Ph.D. *Men Are from Mars, Women Are from Venus: A Practical Guide for Improving Communication and Getting What You Want in Your Relationships.* New York: Harper Collins Publishers, 1992.

———. *Mars and Venus on a Date: A Guide for Navigating the Five Stages of Dating to Create a Loving and Lasting Relationship.* New York: Harper Perennial, 1997.

Hay, Louise L. *You Can Heal Your Life.* Carlsbad, CA: Hay House, Inc., 1984.

Sylvia Ann Hewlett. *Creating a Life: Professional Women and the Quest for Children.* New York: Talk Miramax Books, 2002.

Lerner, Harriet, Ph.D. *The Dance of Anger: A Woman's Guide to Changing the Patterns of Intimate Relationships.* New York: Harper Collins, 1985.

Norwood, Robin. *Women Who Love Too Much: When You Keep Wishing and Hoping He'll Change.* New York: Pocket Books, 1985 (1997).

Peck, M. Scott, M.D. *The Road Less Traveled: A New Psychology of Love, Traditional Values and Spiritual Growth.* New York: Simon & Schuster, 1978.

Peck, Dr. Scott and Shannon. *The Love You Deserve: A Spiritual Guide to Genuine Love.* Solana Beach, CA: Lifepath Publishing, 2002.

Sherven, Judith, Ph.D., and James Sniechowski, Ph.D. *The New Intimacy: Discovering the Magic at the Heart of Your Differences.* Deerfield Beach, FL: Health Communications, Inc., 1997.

Tannen, Deborah. *You Just Don't Understand: Women and Men in Conversation.* New York: Harper Collins, 1990.

## Web sites

Disclaimer—As with all personals type media, the user has to be aware that not everyone on the site is there for the same reason. Some are seriously looking for a long-term partner and others may have other purposes. Please take care of yourself when using the sites by not revealing your personal email addresses or other information before you are comfortable doing so, and most of all, to make sure when meeting a prospective date that it is in a mutually inconvenient and very public space. From an Internet dating specialist: "I did receive a few strange emails over time but nothing too serious to worry about and certainly nothing that stopped me from continuing to look for 'Mr. Right.' I also never met anyone near my apartment and certainly never let anyone walk or drive me home unless I felt truly safe. It is unfortunate, but present times make the issue of safety in dating a priority but it should not make it a deterrent." Please continue to be a smart, self-loving, cautious woman and take responsibility for your safety if you use these sites.

*General sites*   Click on the personals listing and links to web sites on relationships, dating, advice.

www.yahoo.com

www.google.com

www.innerself.com—Articles by therapists, recommended books.

www.searchrelationships.com—Dating portal with search engines, news, chat rooms, links, discussion boards.

www.familyhaven.com—Books, advice, information on Internet dating.

www.about.com—Links, dating services, advice, polls, reader feedback.

www.lovingyou.com—Love, romance, and relationship resources with advice, poetry, quotes, chat, etc.

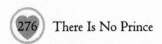

**www.positive-way.com**—New, easy, and proven ways to create positive, lasting, loving relationships.

### Dating Services

Most of these sites have a free introductory offer for the first week or two. They allow you to search and sort by interests, locations, zip codes, area codes, and many more options. They also offer a mailbox so you don't have to publicize your own personal email address.

**www.americansingles.com**

**www.drip.com**

**www.goodgenes.com**—Membership is limited to graduates of certain colleges. The list is on their website.

**www.rightstuffdating.com**—For graduates of top-tier colleges and universities.

**www.kiss.com**

**www.match.com**

**www.matchmaker.com**

**www.singlesonline.com**

**www.jcupid.com**—Jewish Personals

**www.zipple.com**—Jewish Personals

**www.jdate.com**—Jewish Personals (where our Internet specialist met her husband)

**www.singleparentmeet.com**—Good for single parents.

### Dating and mingling events nationwide

**www.datebait.com**—Service providing mixing and mingling evenings for singles with computerized matchmaking.

**www.speeddating.com**—Service providing 8-minute dates and computerized matchmaking. Events are all over the country.

Also look for dating web sites in your area.

# Acknowledgments

To the all men in our lives who taught us what we know about men and most importantly our husbands, the late Vishnu Lee Jayson, and the ever-loving and patient Bill Speers.

The Life Works Guidesses in New York: Patty Accario, Carole Forman, Lisa Gilpin, Paula Kramer Weiss, Sue Krevlin, Sara Lustigman, Sylvia Moss, Miriam Nelson-Gillett, Anne Prather, Gloria Waldman-Schwartz, Peg Warren, Cheryl Marks Young, and Marion Yuen. And those across the country: in Boston: Cathy Petter; Dallas: Susan Lockard and Chris Shull-Caldera; Charlotte, North Carolina: Nancy Schreiber; Philadelphia: Cathy Ellich-Owen; San Francisco: Barbara Blair-Dallosto, and Santa Fe: Debra Cox.

All the graduates of the having "What You Want With a Man" Weekend Workshops who have each contributed their wisdom and energy to the font from which this book flows. To all the guides and teachers who have asked the questions and provided the wisdom that make this work possible.

A special thank-you to women who have supported our work with their own special contributions: Sally Andrews, Debra Cox, Geordie Levitan, Barbara Pettijohn, Marie Prudden, Amanda Rubin, Wendy Sabin-Lasker, and Susan Wallace.

Heartfelt thanks to the team who helped create this book: wordsmiths Caroline Pincus and Elizabeth Law; clarifiers Jeff Braucher, Jackie Boyce, and Nancy Newlin; artists John Buse, Jason Gray, and Paul Mitchell; and Beth Greer, Ellen Kleiner, and Pat Walsh-Haluska for their unfailing generosity and good advice.

To our parents Frances and Maxwell Graman, Michael and Rosemary Walsh, and Catherine Todd and Walter Erston who provided us with rich laboratories as we first explored relationships.

Finally, we thank Swami Satchidananda who taught us that "The rose is itself and the bee comes."

# WOULD YOU LIKE TO HAVE
# YOUR OWN GUIDESS?

You are invited to call Life Works to set up an appointment to speak with a Guidess, one of the wise women whom you read about in this book. Our staff of well-trained women practitioners were called Coaches until several years ago, but the term never fit the delicate and profound work they do. So we invented a new word that we feel more clearly describes the powerful Guiding that they do at Life Works.

Guidesses have completed a three-year training program and are prepared to personally assist you in moving toward what you want by providing weekly support or giving more focused attention on short-term issues. The Guidesses are experts in the Life Works technology and point-of-view. They can partner with you as you begin uncovering and clearing what is in your way, having a stronger, more loving relationship with yourself, clarifying what you want, and gracefully receiving it as it flows into your life.

The Life Works Guiding staff was trained and is supervised by Marilyn and Maureen, and they assist women, men, and couples in private confidential sessions on a weekly or biweekly basis. They work both in person in our New York offices and by telephone to your office or home. The 45-minute sessions are offered at reasonable rates (currently from $40–$85 per session).

We will be glad to assist you in selecting the right Guidess. People who have not completed a Workshop begin with a half-hour intake consultation with our Guidess Coordinator to discuss issues and find the right Guidess match.

If you have been looking to do some work on yourself with a gentle, clear, openhearted, well-grounded woman of wisdom, please call toll-free 877-741-8787 to set up an appointment.

You are invited to join us for the course
that inspired this book.

# You can have the relationship you want

**A successful, fulfilling relationship...**

The "Having What You Want With a Man Workshop" will show you how—whether it means starting from scratch or making the one you have wonderful. The weekend course will give you new insights into men ... and into yourself. It's not just understanding men. It's about being your own best, smart, self-loving self, and maintaining focus so what you truly want can begin to happen. And it's about empowering you to take control when possible and to deal creatively with the array of inevitable relationship issues.

Attractive, intelligent women like you have come out of the workshop surprised to discover the real, underlying issues separating them from what they truly want. With their new insights they see things differently ... which opens them to different thoughts ... different feelings ... which allows them to take different actions.

**It can happen for you.**

Over a weekend Marilyn will show you how to have a successful and satisfying relationship with a man. You will be part of an intense inquiry into how relationships work. You will see how your past, our culture, and other forces have molded your relationships until now.

You will see how taking care of yourself, developing the ability to receive, and exploring women's natural power is crucial to having a good relationship. Finally, we'll have a frank and fun discussion about men—what they're really looking for—and it's not what we've been taught! Marilyn will give you a system for interviewing men and teach you how to transform an OK relationship into a great one. You'll learn how to diagnose problems and start having what you want with a man as never before.

## You can have what you want with a man

### With the right support

Your experience—your work—will stay with you, prompting you to new awareness, perception, and actions. Consciously and unconsciously, you'll be using your workshop experience. And sometimes when you least expect, you will have new insights. If you're like other women, you'll be surprised and delighted that the results of the Workshop will not only help you have what you want with a man but also ripple through your life, enhancing all your relationships, both personal and professional.

### It is possible.

If you long for the strength and compassion of a wonderful man by your side who wants you to be happy, join us for this 2-day course. You can have what you want with a man, and we'll uncover what that means for you in 20 hours. Call 877-741-8787 for details.

## Give Yourself the Gift of a Supportive Relationship

Courses available at Life Works

# WE HELP YOU MAKE YOUR DREAMS COME TRUE...

In the heart of Greenwich Village in downtown Manhattan, Marilyn Graman, Maureen Walsh, and their staff invite you to learn and practice the art of creating and living an invigorating, fulfilling, and meaningful life. A place where you can explore who you are meant to be.

The curriculum at Life Works focuses on the basics—relationships, career, and having more power in your life—in weekly support groups as well as weekend courses and longer retreats and intensives. Underlying all the courses is the conviction that with time, attention, and support, it is possible to unburden your life of the things that haven't been working, while bringing in the things that will give your life more joy, ease, and satisfaction. Through these courses, bright, vibrant, successful people like you are finding a way to more fully express themselves and their own unique nature. Life Works is the home of:

| | |
|---|---|
| **Workshops** | Having What You Want With a Man Weekend* |
| | LifeWorks! Workshop |
| | The Female Power Within* |
| | The Money Workshop |
| | How to Make a Graceful Living |
| | Reboot Your Life—Preparing for the Second Half |
| **Ongoing Groups** | The Gathering* |
| | Relationship Support Group* |
| | Money Support Group |
| **Seminars** | Free and open to guests on the 2nd Wednesday of most months |

| | |
|---|---|
| **Retreats** | Mother* |
| | Father* |
| | Clearing the Path |
| | Manifestation |
| **Intensives** | Marriage Works—A Step-by-step Intensive |
| | Designed to Lead You Down the Aisle* |
| | The Female Power Within Leadership Program* |
| **Guiding Program** | Reasonable rates for weekly private sessions with a |
| | Guidess in person or by phone |
| | * courses for women only |

**From *The New York Times* Money and Business, on Sunday, March 5, 2000:**

"Ms. Graman said the women in her course must first be happy with themselves; she lives by the motto 'the rose is itself and the bee comes.' She does not advise women to change themselves or to deceive men. "We're learning how powerful it can be to be soft and tender. And contrary to popular perception... Manhattan is teeming with men who are eager to tie the knot."

"They're not the enemy," she said. "I see a lot of men in business suits who are longing for a wife, for someone by their side. When the house is empty, they feel lonely. That's why I have no doubt that I can help a woman find a man, because I know there are men out there who want to find her."

**Join us at Life Works and create a life you're glad to wake up to.**

Life Works, Inc.
55 Fifth Avenue—Penthouse
New York, NY 10003
212-741-8787
toll- free 877-741-8787
fax 212-741-9242
Visit our web site: www.lifeworksgroup.com

# More resources from Life Works Books

*There Is NO PRINCE and Other Truths Your Mother Never Told You*
   *—A Guide to Having the Relationship You Want*
ISBN 0-9718548-7-4  Hardbound  $22.95 x_____=_____

*The Female Power Within*
   *—A Guide to Living a Gentler, More Meaningful Life*
ISBN 0-9718548-2-3  Hardbound  $22.95 x_____=_____

*The Female Power Within*
   **Meditation by Marilyn Graman**
meditations from the book plus visualizations
Audio Tape                          $10.00 x_____=_____

"What is the most loving thing I can do for myself now?"
   Heart magnets                    $2.00 x_____=_____

Subtotal  $_____
Tax (New York residents add 8.25%)  $_____
Shipping and handling  $_____
Add $2.95 for first item
and $1.00 for each additional item
Total enclosed  $_____

Make checks or money orders out to:
Life Works Books, and mail to:
Life Works Books
55 Fifth Avenue – Penthouse
New York, NY 10003
www.lifeworksbooks.com

**Watch your bookstore for new Life Works Books releases. Contact us at the address above if you would like to receive our mailings or email us at www.lifeworksbooks.com.**